THE
FASCINATED
OBSERVER

A GUIDE TO
EMBODYING
STAR
PHILOSOPHY

S.T.A.R. Series
Book 2

ALSO BY NINA BROWN

Return of Love to Planet Earth: Memoir of a Reluctant Visionary

S.T.A.R. Philosophy

THE
FASCINATED
OBSERVER

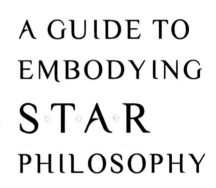

A GUIDE TO
EMBODYING
STAR
PHILOSOPHY

SECOND EDITION

KRISTY SWEETLAND, MTP
& NINA BROWN

SANTA FE, NEW MEXICO

Published by Cauda Pavonis
PO Box 32445
Santa Fe, NM 87594
CaudaPavonisPub.com

Printed in the United States of America

Project development/Editor: Ja-lene Clark
Editors: Jo Ann Deck, Joanne Sprott
Illustrations: Ja-lene Clark
Interior design: Ja-lene Clark
Cover design and interior production: Janice St. Marie
Nina Brown author photo: Lorran Meares, enlight-10.com
Kristy Sweetland author photo: Aaron Tompkins
Art Credit: James E. Jereb's painting *Infinity II—Love*, pages 32–33
Logo: Tammy Mabra

The Fascinated Observer represents the personal and spiritual experiences of the authors. The information in this book is published with the understanding that it is not intended to substitute for professional medical, psychological, legal or financial advice. Neither the publisher nor the authors shall be liable for any physical, psychological, emotional, financial or commercial damages, including, but not limited to, special, incidental, consequential or other damages. If you make use of any of the information in this book, which is your constitutional right, neither the authors nor the publisher assume responsibility for any action you take.

Publisher's Cataloging-in-Publication Data

Names: Sweetland, Kristy, author. | Brown, Nina, 1944- author.
Title: The fascinated observer : a guide to embodying S.T.A.R. philosophy /
                Kristy Sweetland & Nina Brown.
Description: Second edition. | Santa Fe, New Mexico : Cauda Pavonis, [2017] | Series:
                S.T.A.R. series ; book 2.
Identifiers: ISBN: 978-0-9826769-3-6 | LCCN: 2016960976
Subjects: LCSH: Observation (Psychology) | Self-realization. | Self-actualization
                (Psychology) | Interpersonal relations. | Relationship quality. | Well-being.
                | Play--Philosophy. | Play--Psychological aspects. | Ascension of the soul. |
                Spiritual life.
Classification: LCC: BF323.O2 S94 2017 | DDC: 153.7--dc23

CONTENTS

Part Two: Fascinated by Relationships

Willingly Taking Direction from Our Own Divine Self—
A New Level of Confidence

Part Three: The Fascinated Octaves of Wellbeing

Part Four: Playfully Fascinated

Part Five: Quantum Leaps into the Fascinated Observer

*To my cosmic sister, my fairy godmother and
my dear friend Nina Brown. With love and
laughter you delivered my destiny.*

GRATITUDE AND APPRECIATION

First and foremost, my deeply felt appreciation and gratitude are extended to Nina Brown, who pulled me into this incredible experience with the full force of the divine feminine. Strong and loving, you showed me the meaning of divine collaboration.

And to my trio of sacred soul-sisters, Ann Campbell, Shari Southwick and Lynn McGuire-Raj, you were always there for me, always asking questions, wanting to hear more, allowing me to stretch my voice and my wings through the writing of this book. Your unselfish support carried me. I simply adore you.

To my siblings, Jeffrey Sweetland, Tracy Sweetland, Scott Sweetland and Jill Lenzmeier and to my parents who have moved on to the next dimension, my loyalty to you is fierce, my love for you eternal. This love extends to my cherished cats and dogs whose stories are peppered throughout these pages.

I also want to acknowledge my Institute of Transpersonal Psychology family, Karen Gallant, Dr. Patty Hlava, Dr. Henry Poon, Dr. Nancy Rowe, Linda Brown, Mary McKnight, Chelsye Chaney, Bobbi Thompson, Lauretta Zucchetti and Kelly Brant. I wish I had the space to include one hundred more names to this list. You were there when I was becoming my soul-self and were a constant source of love and support.

I want to thank our original editors, Jo Ann Deck and Joanne Sprott, who guided and polished this work with loving mastery, and Ja-lene Clark, who offered great guidance throughout the process.

And finally, to my beloved husband, Aaron Tompkins. You are all things to me, through this world and on to the next. I love you with everything I have.

—Kristy Sweetland

The Fascinated Observer: A Guide to Embodying S.T.A.R. Philosophy fulfills an enormous vision: to see S.T.A.R. philosophy available all around the planet. The goal of this guide is to facilitate that vision.

Profound appreciation to my co-author, Kristy Sweetland. Yours was the life through which the book pulsed into existence. You lived every word you wrote with grace, even when the journey challenged you to stretch into a new skin over and over again. You now walk with mastery and as a model for others for the philosophy of S.T.A.R. and the Four Essential Qualities.

The solid foundation on which this book was placed is due to our S.T.A.R. focus group, which met in the first month of production to discuss key concepts and to shed new light on ideas that now fill the pages of *The Fascinated Observer*. Thank you, Joni Alm, Rick Bastine, Lynne Brosnahan, Patricia Cori, Sara Diaz, Judy Herzl, Barb Retson, Gershon Siegel and Richard Trigg.

Seven years ago, I was introduced to S.T.A.R. by James F. Jereb, PhD, at his magical sacred site, Stardreaming, in Santa Fe, New Mexico. How grateful I am to James for encouraging me to explore the expanded octaves of words that I knew well, *Surrender, Trust, Allow, Receive*. Over the past several years, I have had one "Ah-ha!" after another as new understandings have come to me as I have incorporated S.T.A.R. into my life.

In my first book, *Return of Love to Planet Earth: Memoir of a Reluctant Visionary*, I wrote of that journey and how I stood on my porch one day when the power behind the word surrender became clear to me. It was the ego personality who was to surrender control. The rest fell into place after that, and a book was written focused on those four words. That sounded fun and very easy, for surely it would be a tiny book. The result, *S.T.A.R. Philosophy*, which has touched the lives of so many star seeds around the planet and become a tool for living in and creating a new way of being on planet earth.

Then came another vision: "Let's write a guide to the book so that people can gather in groups to discuss the philosophy and how it applies to everyday life." Into my life popped Kristy Sweetland. Kristy was a new friend, who had read and been so enthusiastic about my first book. I gave her a copy of *S.T.A.R. Philosophy*, when it was hot off the press, to get her initial thoughts. Then we met for lunch to talk about the book. Oh my, her copy was dog-eared and underlined everywhere! She enthusiastically said, "We could use this as teaching material in the institute from which I just graduated." I replied, "Kristy, will you co-author a book with me?" What unfolded from that moment on has been a magical dance, each of us living S.T.A.R. and inspiring the other by means of our experiences.

Let me share with you the new vision that I now hold. My dream is to touch every person on the planet with the S.T.A.R. philosophy. Why? The answer is: We now have a new tool (S.T.A.R.) to dream the new way of being on earth. Now that we have entered the next phase of human evolution—the current 26,000-year cycle, will the old tools serve us? Will the old belief systems continue to support us? Will the way it was create more of the same? Accepting ourselves as sovereign beings, our ego-personality is now safe to *Surrender, Trust, Allow, Receive* all that our human-divinity can dream and imagine and it will be perfect.

—Nina Brown

PREFACE

Divine intervention can take any form; for me, it was delivered in the untidy package of an apparent nervous breakdown. Five years ago I found myself floundering in my own self-made sea of anxiety, stress and discontentment. I had become temporarily disconnected from the philosophy of *Surrender, Trust, Allow, Receive.* Though this philosophy had guided me my entire life, this guidance was synchronized to my relationship with my own soul, which had always been strong. But during the breakdown I became spiritually lost, numbingly disconnected. In a ten-year span, I had moved from Minneapolis to Dallas to the seacoast of New Hampshire, back to Minneapolis. Somewhere along the way I took a bad turn, got confused and forgot who I was. Hard to say where.

I had come to believe that my identity was my career. Having spent nearly twenty successful years in the field of veterinary medicine, it had become all I knew. It was everything to me and was killing me too. I was empathic, intuitive, highly sensitive and worked to bury the constant pain I felt by challenging myself more and more, advancing each of my positions as fast as I could, finally culminating with work in a corporate toxicology center which assisted veterinarians and medical doctors through incidents of accidental poisoning, among other things. My day was spent in a metropolitan high-rise office building managing cases of poisoned animals and documenting the details. This one dies…that one doesn't…this one has horrible suffering…this one not so much. My pain threshold had surpassed its limit a decade before and my resistance to change was clearly tearing me apart.

At the age of nineteen, I lost my mother and for all practical purposes lost my father too, who subsequently surrendered his life to the god of alcohol. It was only my mother who had prevented this downward spiral previously, since my father seemed to have been born with this distilled devil on his back. With her out of the way, there was no halting his course down the path of destruction. He disappeared. I remember being that teen-aged girl, feeling completely alone and allowing the philosophy of S.T.A.R. to guide me, although back then I didn't have a cognitive clue of how it worked. There was no book back then, no tidy container for this omnipresent knowledge. I never used the words, *Surrender, Trust, Allow* or *Receive*, but I lived them.

I have a memory of sitting by myself in an empty playground, my dog seated next to me on a stationary merry-go-round. I slowly dragged my feet, turning the contraption to the right, its glacial speed causing no anxiety for my dog, who lay next to me contemplating the quiet stillness of that grey afternoon. It was autumn and the energy of decay was in the air. My mom had died months earlier, my relationship with my too-young fiancé was falling apart, my dad (likely too drunk to stand) wouldn't answer the door when I knocked on it. I was living in such a state of grief; I had isolated myself from my entire community of friends. As I sat there with my dog, the only creature I hadn't pushed away, I contemplated my belief that I hadn't crumpled under the weight of all of this. I'm not sure back then what my definition of *crumpled* was, but I somehow knew that I had chosen these experiences to become an individual of depth and resilience. By then twenty years old, I looked into the slate sky, crisp-cold in the Minnesota air and mouthed the words, "Thank you" to whoever up there cared to listen, surrendering to this reality I had found myself grieving within. A presence joined me then, a soothing energy, which filled me with the understanding of what it meant to have passion and purpose, the twin driving forces which would come to rule my life. I trusted I would always have them; I knew it and when I strayed too far from their guidance, I would start to wilt, my soul-force severed from the Universal stream of energy which powered me.

To receive, for me, was complicated. It was the energy of receiving that I would have to spend many years mastering, somehow believing I hadn't earned the right yet, always preparing, driving myself through the next accomplishment, dieting, working, earning, accumulating…anything to build the illusion of success without actually building the foundation of self-love, which was the missing piece. It would take me nearly twenty years to integrate this understanding. It would take my life exploding into something terrifying and new before the concept of self-love could begin to rule my life.

Fast forward a couple of decades then and, here I was, now aged thirty-nine, staring my purpose and passion in the face—ignored for so many years—mouthing the words "I'm sorry" to any force willing to listen. I had become so detached from meaning, so lost from presence, that my only reminder of why I was on this planet was sitting in Bloomingdale's bags and hanging in my closet, with the tags of Prada, Christian Dior, Manolo Blahnik, my only justification for existing. If I looked fabulous, I must be doing okay, right? The ego attempts to masquerade when the soul checks out.

But what I learned at the age of thirty-nine was that the soul never truly checks out at all. We may suppress it for months or years, expanding to decades and beyond, but it's always there ready to plug in, the full and beautiful expanse of the Universe waiting to power up with only a moment's notice. At this time in my life and without any warning, my soul blew open illuminating all of the dark shadows in my world. I woke up one morning, ready to go to work and stumbled to the kitchen cupboard, where I kept all of my prescriptions necessary to march through my life like a good soldier. Pills for high-blood pressure, ulcers, depression and anxiety, I stared into that shelf and it became so clear. What the hell was I doing? I was dying here and was too zombified to see the reality. I woke up that day.

Without having any idea what I would do or how we would make ends meet, with my husband's blessing, I quit my job. It had become obvious that it was no longer an option to stay. It was either leave my career and downsize our lifestyle incredibly or die. I felt this on a literal level, my poor body so tired of trying to keep up with the drill sergeant my psyche had become in simply trying to keep me alive, my spirit utterly exhausted. It became clear. I was being asked to surrender like I never had before. Completely surrender. I went to work and gave my notice, so spontaneously I hadn't even informed my best friend in the office that I was considering it. Everyone was stunned. As was I. "What will you do?" they asked me, incredulous at my nonsensical move, fear and concern radiating from their tone. "Are you insane?" one co-worker asked me. I had no idea. I leaped off the cliff, but had no clue where I was meant to land. At that point it didn't matter. I was surrendering my life to my spirit, ready to reconnect, once again giving myself to my passion and purpose without allowing anything to come between us. Not even the false safety of my financial stability, a comfort that had come with a bigger price tag than I could reasonably pay. Had I stayed in that life, I would have died an early death like my mother, in her grave at the age of forty-eight, so detached from her own life-force there seemed to be no igniting it. It was so clear to me.

I worked another two weeks and cleaned out my desk, leaving early in the day and too excited to contain myself. I nearly screamed as I entered the elevator, traveling down four floors to my new life of freedom. I had decided I'd go to California to visit a friend for a couple of weeks, just to clear my head. My friend was going to expand my right-brain creative-in-tuitive side by teaching me how to read Tarot cards, something from which my left-brain analytical side had always kept me. Why not? I wondered. I was unmoored now. It was time to take the straightjacket off and steer this ship anywhere I wanted it to go. I was still riding on adrenaline.

The next morning I awoke to a new, more complicated phase, no longer influenced by the giddy team of endorphins, who had done their cheering and then had gone to sleep. My sleepy eyes focusing on the digital clock beside my bed, illuminated by the early sun—I thought about my work day ahead of me, and then reality hit me. There was no workday ahead of me. A confusing fog of both elation and terror settled over me. No matter how pathologically stressed I had become, I had loved the world of veterinary medicine. When my family fell apart, I threw myself into my work, allowing it to become a place of refuge. Animals for me had always been my saviors, my cherished teachers and beloved guides; they still are. But I had stopped fitting in to the politics of the industry a full decade before I left it. I didn't align with what the majority believed in any longer—the fear tactics, the chemicals, the constant vaccines—though there were many in the industry who felt exactly as I did. There was an intuitive side of me which believed in animal communication, psychic phenomenon, channeling, oddities that I could never reveal in my industry, not any place I had worked anyways. For twenty years I pretended to be something I was not, allowing the analytical side of me to rule, in order to conform to our society's standards.

Choosing to see the world as intolerant was my choice entirely. I chose to not share myself with those around me. They were beautiful people; I could have given them more credit. I had completely lost sight of my own divinity, too afraid to forge my own path; like so many others, I chose perceived conformity. Now, it seemed, my being was demanding integration, all exiled parts of me asking for reentry, demanding it. My life depended on it. My soul was speaking to me so clearly, my heart beating so purely, every one of my cells inhaling and exhaling a new sense of freedom so energizing, I couldn't let fear dictate my next move. My body wouldn't allow it. I had already surrendered, it was time to trust and I did that too.

Allowance for me came with greater resistance. I left for California early morning, mid-week, my ten-month old Saluki puppy my copilot on my trip across country. My objective was to detox the past twenty years from my system and to find a new clean slate from which to begin again. I thought this new start would take place with my Tarot card lessons in Los Angeles; my sadly contained ego felt at the time that this was the most outrageous activity I could participate in.

I would soon find that the Universe had different plans for me, so wildly beyond anything I could have imagined, that my psyche would be nearly split in two. Driving through the serene and well-behaved states of Iowa, Nebraska and Colorado, my life took a turn for the outrageous as soon as I crossed the border of the Land of Enchantment. New Mexico roared alive, demons and angels dragging me into an alternate dimension the moment my wheels rolled over the state line. I never made it to California. For ten days I wandered the highways of this fantastical place in an altered state, experiencing too many mind-blowing encounters with people, living and dead, to document, learning what it meant to allow new energies into my life. I fell into the collective conscious, started hearing animals speak and heard telepathic conversations so loudly it was as if I had a wire in my ear. I saw dead people frozen in time, wax statues peppered about the country-side, in stores, on streets. The living walked right through them, around them, but nobody saw them except me. I wondered if this was to be my fate, this wax statue existence, had I not broken from my severe pattern of prescription pills and soul-numbing stagnancy.

Through all of this, I was forced to question everything I knew. I learned how many illusions in our world keep us imprisoned and contained, safe and orderly. I learned how imperative it was to believe in our own divinity, our own magnificence capable of so much love. I learned how important it was to follow the joy in life as a constant guide and to live present in every moment. And I learned what I had always known, but with much greater clarity, that when we hurt each other and treat each other with disrespect—and that means all of us in the form of fellow humans, animals, insects, rocks, trees, flowers...we are all sentient beings—we are causing the demise of not only ourselves but the entire world. I allowed all of this in, these divine teachings serving as medicine to heal my exhausted soul. I visited Heaven in New Mexico, I visited Hell and each one was right inside of me all along.

Those ten days were both awesome and awful. I vacillated between pure ecstasy and sheer terror. I felt like I was losing my mind, being torn apart, annihilated, all of which were necessary for me to reintegrate all parts of myself. Somehow I drove myself back home, four states away, to Minneapolis. Once I arrived, it took me several weeks before I could be around people again, feeling gooey and newborn like a butterfly just out of her cocoon. I felt like I was going to die. I couldn't watch television, couldn't listen to music; if ever I was confronted by any low-vibrational or negative energy I would literally vomit. I was becoming something new.

In addition to my schooling in the veterinary field, at the time I also had a bachelor's degree in psychology. I knew enough to know that what was happening to me didn't fit any textbook diagnosis. I was hearing telepathic voices but they were not self-aggrandizing or paranoid. It was like being tapped into a Zen master, receiving teachings on different aspects of myself and how they were influenced and driven by the world around me. If this was schizophrenia, it wasn't like anything anyone has ever written about. What the hell was happening to me? I didn't feel safe checking with any psychotherapist I knew. My instinct was, the average cognitive-behavioral therapist would have no understanding.

So, I went on a mad search to find for myself what had happened to me, what *was still* happening to me. I read everything Eckhart Tolle had written and everything Stanislav and Christina Grof had written on the *Spiritual Emergency*. I read *Trials of the Visionary Mind* by John Weir Perry and *Broken Open* by Elizabeth Lesser. Because my experience in New Mexico was clearly shamanic, I read every classic and modern book on shamanism I could get my hands on. I read these and dozens more, anything that would shed light on what I had gone through during those ten terrifying days in New Mexico. I found psychological dissertations online from transpersonal psychology graduate programs. Through all of my reading I found story after story of experiences exactly like mine. I wasn't crazy after all. I had experienced what the transpersonal psychology world refers to as a spiritual emergency in the form of a spontaneous shamanic initiation, brought on by many years of repressing an entire hemisphere of my brain, and the experience of so much stress and so much trauma over my life-time. All of it was released, broken open, with my sudden decision to leave my career, which was the only identity I had known. Whereas many people have a gradual spiritual emergence, others just blast open all at once, blowing all of their psychic circuits in one nuclear-caliber explosion. People go crazy through these experiences. People die from these experiences. As for me, it took me three years to fully integrate what I had experienced in the desert of New Mexico.

Within six months of having this event take place in my life, my husband and I moved to Raton, New Mexico, a tiny mountain town on the border of Colorado. Not knowing if New Mexico was some kind of portal to alternate dimensions for me, I think we chose to stay close to the Colorado border, clinging to its quiet strength and less volcanic energy, for my psychological safety. We had no idea what to expect. In the foothills of the Rocky Mountains with no distractions and no frenzied metropolitan stimulus, I completed a master's degree in transpersonal psychology. For me, it revealed itself to be my life's calling. Helping people through these wild rides of spiritual emergence, something happening to millions of people every day across the world at a rate that is increasing exponentially, is why I chose to be born at this incredible juncture of our planetary history.

When I first met Nina Brown, she looked at me with those deeply penetrating eyes and said; "Who. Are. You?"—her focus eager, intent on my answer. I froze. A half smile involuntarily formed as I glanced around, waiting to be rescued by the existential police force, a figment of my desperate imagination. The question made me supremely uncomfortable. Her focus remained. "I have no idea how to answer that question," I offered, not because I felt I didn't know, but I felt that I didn't know what she wanted to hear and I so wanted to please her! It was like taking an impromptu test I hadn't studied for, something that just doesn't happen in my world! The truth is, nobody had ever asked me this question before—not like this. Who am I? This preface is my attempt at answering the long version of this question. In short, I am a comet, blazing my way across the Universe, bringing light into darkness, hoping to encourage others to do the same.

This opening dialogue between Nina and me has become my North Star and the reason I'm co-authoring this book. I have come to believe that the question, "Who are you?" is the key to manifesting the new paradigm for our planet earth. It was Barbara Marciniak who said, "Everything changes when you start to emit your own frequencies rather than absorbing the frequencies around you, when you start imprinting your intent on the Universe rather than receiving an imprint from existence." Imagine how our world would change if we all lived this as truth? My belief is that Nina Brown has given us a map to decode this truth. To understand the Four Essential Qualities of the S.T.A.R. philosophy, which are *Wholeness (human divinity)*—we are the masters of our own reality, we are the creators of our own experiences, *Self-love*—we can't know what it means to love until we learn to love ourselves, *Play (the now moment)*— living in the now and all the joy it holds and the *Embodiment of the Expanded Golden Rule*—do unto all creation as we would have done unto us, is to build the foundation for this work. Once we have arrived at a place where we can live this philosophy, only then can we begin to know what it means to *Surrender, Trust, Allow, Receive* all that the Universe is so eager to deliver.

The journey of writing this book has been a total immersion into the totality of this philosophy. Writing it required that I become a Universal case study for encoding and imprinting its power into these words, onto these pages. Through this writing experience I temporarily lost sight in one eye, hearing in one ear and had spiritual and emotional experiences so intense I felt like I was literally being carried through the eye of chaos. And then stillness. Only to repeat again and again through each chapter. Through it, that sweet guidance—*Surrender, Trust, Allow, Receive*—kept me walking forward, into my own transformation, which finds me at a place of supreme gratitude for all things, no matter how difficult, intense love for those in my life, no matter what they're here to teach me and a near constant evaluation of where my own judgment is holding me back and holding me down, rather than leading me forward. This incredible transformation for me finally culminated in a total spiritual declaration to be here now, in this body, on this earth as a fierce, loving, perfectly divine human being, here to learn from every experience and move into a higher octave of knowing, loving, learning and purpose.

The journey of reading this book will be whatever your soul needs it to be. Sweet, shocking or subtle, your experience will be perfectly orchestrated to receive the desires of your soul. I lived the book to write the book, so I could share it with you today. This act, I believe, is the culmination of my lifelong quest—my soul-level calling, dreams and purpose. With great love I offer this body of writing. Use it in your own exquisite ways on the path to realizing your dreams.

—Kristy Sweetland

How Do I Use This Book?

Through the pages of this book we invite you to be the Fascinated Observer of your own life. This means navigating through the lenses of learning, loving and discerning without resorting to harsh judgment, in keeping with S.T.A.R. principles. S.T.A.R. philosophy is a nondogmatic collection of insights and ideas, meant as a baseline from which to build a completely empowered existence. There are no instructions, only suggestions. We encourage you to mold these ideas into a form that is perfectly adapted to you.

While reading this book and applying it to your own life, we encourage you to take any expectations of receiving a one-size-fits-all "how to" instruction for a perfect life and lovingly discard those thoughts. There is no "how it should be" with this guide, only words selected to lead you to find what feels right for you. If you want to do every activity listed, fabulous. If you want to skip around and read sections that feel relevant to you right now, do it! Use it like an oracle and think of a question and open your book to a random page. How you read it is up to you. You are an exquisite divine being that is totally capable of making excellent decisions. During and after reading, we encourage you to listen to your intuition and all of your senses to find what works for you. If you find you would like to do this work in conjunction with the work of a therapist or a transformational coach or a healer of any kind, please follow your own lead. You know the way.

Find your tribe or let your tribe find you. No matter what your philosophical slant is, human brilliance is accelerated through group activity. The chapters in this book are written for the individual, but we set an intention to design the work to be perfectly suited for group activity as well. We encourage you to gather with others to discuss your experiences as the Fascinated Observer.

This book is about the recognition of divinity inside of us as well as all around us. Our desire is that you take an empowered approach to using this book and please have *fun* with it. It's meant to be light as well as powerful.

The words within these chapters are encoded with a transformative energy signature. We the authors have embedded our own personal experiences of becoming Fascinated Observers into the pages. We lived it, we experimented, we tested the formulas and now we can share it. We offer insights to inspire you sprinkled with activities to give you ideas on how to apply the *The Fascinated Observer* to your life. We're right here with you on your fascinating journey of *Surrender, Trust, Allow, Receive.*

S.T.A.R. Philosophy Key Terms

Definition of the Words

within the Term "S.T.A.R."

S.T.A.R.: When one aligns with the will
and love of universal source energy

SURRENDER to the tranquility of
knowing human divinity

TRUST in wholeness to express

ALLOW human divinity to evolve

RECEIVE with appreciation and gratitude

PHILOSOPHY IS:

THE ACTIVITY THROUGH WHICH WE SEE CREATION THROUGH THE EYES OF ONENESS.

The full octave expression of philosophy is about nurturing the seeds of wisdom hibernating in our sacred hearts. We are born with those seeds. The philosopher's stone, that holds the secret seeds to everything, has transformed into the philosopher's seed—a living being which can burst forth into new, never before expressed shapes and forms with playful creativity.

THE ESSENTIAL QUALITIES OF THE

S.T.A.R. PHILOSOPHY

WHOLENESS (human divinity)

SELF-LOVE

PLAY (the now moment)

EMBODIMENT OF THE EXPANDED GOLDEN RULE

Throughout this book you will frequently see the word *octave* used in place of descriptives such as *level, higher* or *degree.* We do this to avoid the implication of any hierarchical measure of spiritual progression. *The Fascinated Observer's* message is this: Wherever we are on our journey is perfect. There is no journey "more advanced" or superior to another's just as any musical masterpiece shows us that every note, high or low, is critically important to the piece.

I Am the Author of My Reality

by Nina Brown

(To be read aloud)

Who am I?
I am a being of light.
My light is brighter
than I have thought.
I surrender
to the light I am.

Who am I?
I am a divine,
sovereign being
experiencing from
the perception
of my human body.

Who am I?
I am the source of creation.
I am the created.
I am a valuable part of
All That Is.

As a creator being,
what do I choose to create?
I choose to create
one experience
at a time in each now moment.
I choose to live what
I have created with no
judgment.

SURRENDER TRUST ALLOW RECEIVE

THERE IS NO OTHER
TRUTH THAN I AM LOVE.

RECEIVE ALLOW TRUST SURRENDER

Instead, I am
the Fascinated Observer.

SURRENDER TRUST ALLOW RECEIVE

I choose to have
appreciation and gratitude
for each experience
and I trust the magic
that it brings.

I choose to allow
each created experience
to flow into me,
through me and out from me
bringing love
to all it touches.

LOVE IS SOURCE
MANIFESTING IN ME.

SURRENDER TRUST ALLOW RECEIVE

I choose to be an ambassador
beaming out the Embodiment
of the Expanded Golden Rule.

Who am I?
I am love.
I am the author of my reality.
I am fascinated.
I choose my reality into
being as an expression
of the light and
love that I am.

PART ONE:
FASCINATED BY RICHNESS

THE FASCINATED OBSERVER

From *S.T.A.R. Philosophy* by Nina Brown (pages 127–130)

On the Fascinated Observer, the following section introduces this idea:

With "fascination" is the most empowered manner in which the observer experiences the soul's journey on the spiral of life. From the vantage point of fascination, one is participating in what is presented—from experiences, to events, to conversations and in relationships, with the delight of watching what shows up. Fascination allows one to ask, "Wow, why did I create that experience?"

As an observer of one's life, circumstances lose their power to effect negative emotions. My favorite example is when one goes to the supermarket and stands behind a person who has eleven items in the ten-items-only, check-out aisle. The typical reaction is to hold an internal dialogue that goes something like this, "He ought to go back to school and learn how to count!!!!!! I'm going to be late for my dog grooming appointment. How could he do this to me?"

The situation is really all about us. Why am I getting so disturbed? Why am I feeling this way? The event, whatever it might be, just is. It is how we react to it that is causing thought, feeling and behavior. A different way to respond, as the observer, to seeing eleven grocery items in front of you, is to ask, "How is my life going to be different because of this perceived delay?" Could it be that you are still in the store when your best friend enters?

Perhaps being put on a different time schedule allowed you to miss a negative event that you would have been involved in had you exited earlier. Or did the quiet time standing in line allow you to have an "Ah-ha!" thought that would not have occurred had you rushed out the door?

To expand on this thought, let me share a personal experience which happened in the Santa Fe post office. The time was about ten o'clock and the line of customers was unusually long. I [Nina] had an overnight letter to post, so leaving was not an option. The woman two people ahead of me had a shopping cart filled with what seemed like thirty-five boxes. I learned from overhearing her conversation, how she sold her products through eBay, the online shopping and auction network and this was her second visit to the post office that day.

While I was standing in the line, which turned out to be for a little under an hour, I shifted my mind to the question, "Why am I in such a slow line, just standing here?" Then a thought came to me, "Stand up straight." Curious, I pulled my shoulders back and held a very erect posture. The muscles in my back began to ache, but I held firmly. Then I remembered that I had spent the last week crouched on a sofa watching hours and hours worth of the 2012 Olympic Games being televised from London, England. No wonder my posture was poor. After a half hour, the muscles stopped hurting and it felt natural to stand so straight. What had possibly seemed like a disruption to the flow of my day had turned out to be a gift in disguise.

To be an observer in the octaves of S.T.A.R. removes judgment. The eBay vendor was not wrong. The line of people wishing to use the postal service was not wrong. The event that appeared in my life just was. One might call this mode of observing a form of innocent perception: to be aware without bias.

For example, when we meet a person wearing a black leather jacket, it is easy to assume that they are a motorcycle rider. Innocent perception allows us to merely observe that the jacket is black and leather, without assigning a quality, characteristic and behavior to the person choosing to wear the jacket. We are merely allowing the identity or personality of the individual to unfold. We know that, under all the signs and symbols, we might observe that the true identity of the person that we have just met is an individual aspect of All That Is expressing and experiencing in a unique way.

Another way to be an observer is to be aware of our bodies. How does the environment and linear time affect our emotional responses? When we notice how thoughts make us feel, then we are able to reflect on those thoughts and choose to make a different choice if signs of physical discomfort are present. While daydreaming, I had a thought about a project I was involved in. I noticed that my body tightened up as I projected that thought into the future. I was noticing my physical response to the emotion of fear. I took my thought out of future time and moved it into my sacred heart, the now, and the feeling disappeared. I chose to dream about the event and to see it occurring in a manner that gave me delight. My feelings shifted to a calm sense of joy. I saw myself and all the participants involved in the project. All was unfolding beautifully. Then I asked the question: "Is there an action step for me to take to facilitate the successful outcome of my dream?" The answer was: "Let go. Surrender, Trust, Allow, Receive what it is that you have imagined with appreciation and gratitude." My will was aligned with the will of the divine Creator. The event would express perfectly.

CHAPTER ONE:
THE MANY FORMS OF RICHNESS

RICHNESS IS A FABULOUS WORD. Though we may instantly associate the term with financial fortune, truly here we are extending beyond the scope of our material life. Our collective beliefs surrounding the subject of work or career and abundance have been confusing. As children we may have been encouraged to overlook passion and purpose as frivolous. There are a lot of pressures to conform, to do whatever it is that "successful people do." We have to make a living, right? The real confusion enters when we hear feedback that diminishes the power of our personal dream of making that living; "You want to be a musician? A poet? You'll starve to death! Find something else to do where you can actually make money." Being barraged with these beliefs can be hurtful. Succumbing to them can lead us straight to a path of:

1. Agreeing that our dreams are a symptom of childhood whimsy.

2. Denying the call of our soul.

3. Giving in to the energy of words like "sensible, lucrative and respectable," which are each beautiful yet contain elements of lack when used to discourage the path of others.

4. Not realizing that sensible, lucrative and respectable can be gracefully merged with the concepts of passion, purpose and trailblazing, no matter how outlandish our dreams.

5. Finding ourselves in a world so stifled that harmless words like "safety and security" become synonymous with "prison, suffocation, settling, responsibility and boredom."

6. Forgetting our dreams entirely.

The S.T.A.R. philosophy is a beacon that leads us to the path our soul chose long before our birth. We can have it all! We can cross the line. If we desire to create new situations in our life, we absolutely can—we can choose to create richness at its most exquisite octave. If fulfilling our purpose means making a living doing what we love, then let's go! Fascinated Observers can choose in any moment to gracefully change paths. But if we desire to truly surpass what we have been able to create up to this very point in time, we must leave the now to meet our *little self* with the intention of gaining help in remembering what we once wanted. The imagination we possessed as children holds insights for us to harvest right now.

Here's how to start:

1. Find a picture of you when you were in kindergarten, first or second grade.

2. Concentrate on that image to connect with your little self.

3. Find at least three things that you like about that photo of you. For example; your hair or smile or something sweet you remember about that day.

Fill in the blanks to answer the following questions.

When I was little I wanted to:

When I was little I was told that success is:

I thought being rich meant:

I believed I would be successful if:

When I was little I thought abundance was:

When I was little the thing I thought was best about me was:

When I was little the thing I was most afraid of was:

I told myself that when I got bigger I would:

I wish I could go back and tell myself:

I used to imagine I would:

After you have contemplated, let go. Wait for new insight. When it comes, receive your own personal "Ah-ha!" Sit with that insight and then:

1. Move into present time and write your own journal entry, poem, essay or paint an image that shows how you wish to envision your responses from now on, according to what this new insight has taught you.

2. Complete the following sentence:

Now that I accept my divinity, I believe richness to me is

Let's take the past, use it as fuel and create something new in this moment.

REDEFINING OUR BELIEFS

We almost called this chapter "work and prosperity," however, as we wrote about this subject, the subject started rewriting our lives and redefining our beliefs in the most extraordinary ways. The journey of writing this chapter took us deep within to observe the source of where our shared beliefs about work and prosperity originated. We wondered why we near-robotically associated work with wealth and prosperity with material goods or a means to attain material goods or comforts? They say, "You can't take it with you." This is true with material wealth. But we believe that we DO take the riches from our spiritual and relational experiences with us when we leave our physical body behind. With our beliefs refocused, we began to realize our enormous riches could be easily segmented into three major categories:

1. Our material riches

2. Our spiritual riches

3. Our relational riches

Our material riches are one facet of our life. Without activating our intention to fully develop all three, is our life truly rich? Our spiritual riches bring dimension to our life; they bring us depth and grace. Our relational riches offer us a foundation of love and support. They carry us through the dark times; they create our community. Creating dialogue with all three facets brings us to a rich foundation from which to build our lives.

In *S.T.A.R. Philosophy*, Nina wrote about prosperity, which is our link into the octave of richness: "Will daily existence be a struggle or could we dream into existence all that we need to support us in achieving that which we came to earth to accomplish? Will what is manifested always be the comfort that the personality struggles for? What is the definition of prosperity in the new way of being on earth? One way to find the answer might be to project oneself to the last day of physical expression on the planet. When we have the vantage point of looking back, what do we hold as valuable? Would it be the money that we have earned? Would it be the "stuff" that we have collected? Perhaps not, perhaps we might hold most valuable the relationships with our family, friends and neighbors and the experiences through which we have traveled."

Sit with that passage from Nina for a moment. Let the ideas settle and then ask yourself, "What is *my* definition of richness? Where do I want more richness in my life?"

Throughout this book we will encourage you to master asking questions. As divine humans we observe, ponder, consider and contemplate to gather insights for making empowered choices. Great philosophers throughout history have mastered the action of asking excellent questions. Unlike what we have been trained to do in the past, we do not exclusively seek "the answer," instead we choose to make quantum leaps. This book was created with love as a guide (rather than a rote must-follow-all-directions-precisely formula) for its readers to start taking those leaps on your own, as sovereign beings. Contemplation, along with feeling, is a perfect starting point. You don't need a guru; we're here to offer you an invitation for your own inner exploration.

Activity: The Richness Contemplation

Take as much time as you wish to fully integrate and contemplate the following questions:

- ◎ What does abundance mean to ME?

- ◎ What is money?

- ◎ What is prosperity?

Contemplate the three types of prosperity. Then ask yourself, "With which kind do I enjoy the greatest abundance? And in which do I desire to grow"?

- ◎ Material prosperity

- ◎ Spiritual prosperity

- ◎ Relational prosperity

Additional questions:

- ◎ Why do abundance, prosperity and money matter to me?

○ What do I perceive to be in my way of abundantly receiving what I choose to receive?

○ What do I choose to dream?

○ Is financial wealth my choice?

○ Is having all the time I desire to spend with my kids, pets, family or friends what I choose?

○ Is sharing depth and connection with as many friends as I can possibly fit into my life important to me?

○ Is my prosperity expressed through my beautiful surroundings?

○ Is it being able to afford travel or adventure?

○ What do I really need? Have I declared my needs to the Universe?

PONDER...

Then when you feel complete, ask yourself:

○ How do I describe and define richness?

Now that is F A S C I N A T I N G, right?

Richness is within EVERYTHING! Is there a voice anywhere within you that says you can't decide for yourself what richness means? You define your world. Make the choice to grow into your dreams, no matter how immense they may seem! Here larger is better. Observe, dream and grow. After exploring those questions, be prepared and open yourself to receive something new.

APPRAISING OUR ASSETS

In *S. T.A.R. Philosophy* Nina wrote about financial health, which is synonymous with prosperity. When we are willfully living our financial and professional wholeness we can:

Surrender our anxiety to the tranquility of our own internal power.

Trust that the flow of our assets is divinely orchestrated.

Allow lack or plenty to express at our command.

Receive all of life's experiences with inner calm.

What would it take to embody these concepts? Where do you find yourself resisting or doubting? Take a moment to observe your thoughts on the S.T.A.R. philosophy as they relate to your perceptions about richness. Simply witness your process with the eyes of a Fascinated Observer.

Once we have started to play with the S.T.A.R. philosophy, perhaps no other area of life challenges us more ferociously than in the areas of work, abundance and prosperity which all dovetail into the word *richness*. Even when we have consciously claimed our human divinity and welcomed the joy of abundance, unconscious thought patterns can creep right back into our everyday experience. We may slide into worries and fears especially where we have in the past been vulnerable—perhaps about security, stability, compensation, fulfillment and self-worth—then suddenly observe that those thoughts are dominating and tampering with our present intentions. Even after we've incorporated the ideas of *Surrender, Trust, Allow, Receive* into our daily life, we may forget that we are divine, sovereign beings who have chosen to experience precisely the richness of all that we are enmeshed in.

Practicing S.T.A.R. can seem challenging if we're perpetually concerned about paying the bills or keeping up with the demands of our many roles. Most of us are driven by a desire to experience fulfillment in all areas of life—especially with work and prosperity! The challenge, according to a recent study, is that 54% percent of Americans are only mildly satisfied to very unsatisfied with their current work (University of California Berkeley, 2012). Why do so many of us strive for nothing greater than mild satisfaction? That's no fun. Can we be at play when we're working at our job? Yes, we absolutely can.

There are those who leap out of bed each morning eager to start their day, understanding that abundance comes in myriad forms and not necessarily connected to a paycheck, college degree or winning the lottery. These divine beings are guided by the internal compass of passion and purpose, understanding that prosperity extends beyond the concept of money. They know where to go, when to go and seem to effortlessly follow the direction of a divine master plan. You know these people. They radiate light and energy, their very presence raises the frequency of those around them, the Universal flow coursing through their every action. It does not matter how they "make a living," they exude richness. When they disappear, off one week for a trip to the Bahamas, those they've left behind droop in their absence. What do they have that seems elusive? We may have heard the sarcastic responses when a workmate comes bouncing in the door each morning enthusiastically chirping her good mornings. "What's she on?" "I want some of that." "Who put what in her coffee?"

Putting S.T.A.R. to work in your life might look something like this:

- SURRENDER and plug into the Universal stream of abundance

- TRUST and believe it

- KNOW you are a divine creator being

- OWN it and feel it in your body as if it has already taken place

- ALLOW it to be what it is…perfect

- OBSERVE with fascination when you slip out of abundance and then snap out of it

- ACCEPT it

- RECEIVE it and express gratitude

The truth is there is no external power source, elusive to our reach. Each one of us has an opportunity to generate the energy needed to propel onward to experience all the richness life has to offer. Being a divine human is an exquisite opportunity to do just that. Receiving richness is neither elusive nor complicated; they are achieved through observation of self—becoming the Fascinated Observer. That begins with your divine choice as a sovereign human being.

RECLAIMING OUR DIVINITY

The effects of forcing ourselves into a pattern of prolonged stagnancy, professional or otherwise, to achieve the definition we were trained as a child to believe is "success" are widespread. This can be a trap. The fear of lack and the fear of moving forward are simple textures to observe on the path to the journey of wholeness. We can identify new fulfilling ways to bring that paycheck home to our families. The notion that there's no time to reset and readjust our path because we need to maintain our lifestyle is just a belief we may have agreed upon, a belief we made the choice to transcend at some point in our soul's evolution. Our families depend on us to be vibrant, fulfilled and joyful much more than they need our paychecks. We Trust that abundance comes in myriad forms, and that richness is not limited to finances, and yet we can find ourselves plugging away at a job or career we've outgrown due to our fear of change. The truth is, the very change we fear we can't "afford" may lead us to greater financial riches than we previously enjoyed. It happens all the time, actually.

To enter the state where new possibilities can begin to take shape, we can use S.T.A.R. to access our power. When we add to that the application of the Four Essential Qualities, quantum leaps become possible. For example, in the area of richness, what do you observe when you connect the words richness and wholeness? The addition of that simple word gives us the ability to start to see new images forming; a whole new energy emerges. That's fascinating!

Wholeness in surrendering to our human divinity means that we take full responsibility for our own sovereignty. We disconnect from any desire to blame or punish others around us for the state our life is in. It's a no drama zone when we accept that we are each divine creators, makers of our own reality. We are not victims of circumstance or misfortune. All of the experiences we manifest in our lives are priceless information, here to deliver the building blocks as stepping-stones to our own evolution. When we spend our time and effort focusing on the judgment of others (that person is not loving me enough), hiding behind our own perceptions (life is perpetually unfair; I will always be broke) and relinquishing our power (I can't create change in my life because I'm a victim of destiny) then a miracle takes place. We find ourselves perpetually stuck behind the energy of neglect, victimization and powerlessness. We make it our reality! Our energy becomes our truth. Our truths create our perceptions of the world. Claiming our human divinity means no longer accepting that we are helpless creatures, victims of unfair circumstance over which we have no control.

WE ARE EACH A DIVINE CREATOR BEING

Accepting our human divinity is quite a leap. Acceptance means that we start to look at the landscape of our life from a vantage point that can see usefulness in both the beautiful and challenging circumstances we experience. This takes an octave leap in objectivity. We understand that we have chosen our life experiences for any number of valuable reasons.

Perhaps we:

O Wanted to know what it feels like to be stuck doing something we dislike, because we know we have the power to initiate great change in our life to remedy it.

O Knew that the displeasure of an unsatisfactory work experience was necessary so that we may transcend the belief that our work defines our life.

O Want to learn to observe the difficulties we find within our life as gifts used to grow and transform into something stronger and more vital.

O Required ground-level insights that came from understanding what doesn't work in our chosen profession, so we can fully align with what does and adapt out-dated systems on planet earth.

We have "bad" experiences for good reasons. We are expansive, radiant, divine beings who have complete sovereignty over the direction of our lives. Our soul holds a level of wisdom that the human mind is challenged to comprehend. The human mind usually understands the value of a challenging experience with hindsight, while our divinity has the foresight to lead us through the mud and muck into the most exquisite places.

PLAY WITH NEW OCTAVES

Recently, I (Kristy) decided to bring my coaching practice to a new octave. I was ready to work with a much larger number of clients, so I committed to further developing my business. I was expending a lot of energy; at times it no longer felt fun.

What was happening, I wondered? Looking back, I realize that I became too focused on the material, at the expense of my spiritual and relational richness. It was beginning to feel forced. But at the time, it wasn't so clear. I loved my coaching, which usually brings with it an inexhaustible amount of energy for me.

> COULD YOU BE "BANKRUPT" IF YOU HAVE SPIRITUAL AND RELATIONAL RICHNESS?

Enter my brother-in-law, who shifted things with one simple statement. Without having a clue that I was struggling, he called me one morning. What he said to me caused an octave shift that entirely altered the course of my work.

First of all, he praised my writing. I love my brother-in-law immensely and we're from two very different worlds. He's an executive for a huge corporate chain of home improvement stores in the country, living in Atlanta, conservative, analytical and has the biggest heart of anyone I know. It always thrills me to hear he enjoys my stuff because I write from such an alternative platform. When he tells me it resonates, it really means something to me. On this particular day, he wanted to share some wisdom. He told me, "You think of yourself as a coach who works to get clients so you can have the privilege to write. I want you to instead think of yourself as a writer whose work generates all of your coaching clients." That was it. Wait. What?!

One tiny shift in perception blew me wide open. My analytical side tells me I have impressive credentials as a coach, but do I have the creative right to call myself a writer, I wondered? "Hell yes, I do!" I responded. I made a Universal declaration. "I am a writer, whose writing generates my coaching business!" I said it over and over because it felt so right, so decadent! Instantly, my energy returned to me. The next day, I had a lunch date with Nina Brown, who asked me to co-write this book. Enter my odyssey.

First, align with my Four Essential Qualities:

○ In accepting my *Wholeness (human divinity)* I knew that I created my own reality.

○ In embracing my *Self-love* I knew that I fully believed in myself to follow my dreams with no doubts or fear. I knew that my joy required a balance of my material, spiritual and relational richness.

○ By living in *Play (the now moment)*, I understood that only this moment is "real" and by using my joy to guide me, I knew I was on the perfect path.

○ And by being in the *Embodiment of the Expanded Golden Rule*, I connected with my soul purpose which is to bring re-connection to passion, freedom of expression and authenticity of spirit to every person my work touches, which in turn brings healing to the entire planet.

And then I was ready to:

○ *Surrender* to my divine will. My soul-purpose is to write books.

○ *Trust* that all was happening perfectly.

○ *Allow* myself to flow into the possibilities opening up for me without getting in my own way with self-doubt or fear.

○ *Receive* the writing contract (the very next day).

DISTILLING YOUR ANSWERS

Can you feel a new blueprint for richness forming within you? Material, spiritual and relational riches ARE our divine birthright and are there for us when we make the decision to receive them in our lives. Through these pages, we hope you've distilled YOUR answers to the questions, "What do I desire?

What do I need?" in this lifetime, in relation to your riches. There is no single absolute answer. Our answers are an individual experience, yet for all of us clarification is where the practice begins.

Chapter Two:
Riding the Flow of Richness

TO WRITE THIS BOOK, I (Kristy) had to make the space for it in my life. That meant pulling out of other projects for which I was earning money but for which I had no enthusiasm. I realized that those projects drained me rather than energized me. I knew this wasn't sustainable, so I made the decision to empty my schedule for nothing more than my writing and my coaching. My love of self was stronger than my need for "security." I chose to live the ideas of S.T.A.R. and trusted the money would flow. This was a real test of my beliefs. It took several weeks to tie up all the loose ends and then, breathing a big sigh of relief, I took a week of vacation to recharge and regenerate prior to entering this new phase of my life.

The week came for me to step into my new role as author/coach with no additional distractions. There were only tiny hints of fear; I had given up steady income to make this shift, but the S.T.A.R. philosophy had become such a way of being for me that I worked to transform the remaining fear into fuel I could use for this new exciting venture. I made the space and my dreams manifested. That first week one of the top coaches in the country completely out of the blue offered to mentor me, and I began to manifest other forms of riches practically in my sleep. I had a conversation with my husband that centered around my desire to see the Santa Fe Opera's production of *La Traviata,* and the next day an offer for incredibly discounted tickets arrived from a friend just feeling I'd be interested. I purchased $500 worth of opera tickets for $30. Then I wanted to attend an upcoming workshop, but thought it might not be sensible for me to spend the money at the time. Without so much as whispering a word to anybody, an offer immediately dropped in my lap for me to take the workshop at half price, something I could easily afford. That week I received eight new clients into my coaching practice, which, prior to then, had never happened in the history of my coaching. I'm telling you, this was incredible stuff for me.

Nature abhors a vacuum. We make the space, practice the S.T.A.R. philosophy and magic happens.

The essential quality, *Self-love*, dreams our new life into being. That quality was particularly enmeshed with my choice to change paths, as was my understanding of *Wholeness (human divinity)*.

Without a solid connection to our own magnificence and worth, we sell ourselves short, stay in lives too small and forget that we deserve whatever beautiful circumstance we can imagine. There are so many stories of men and women being stuck behind the memory of a domineering parent or teacher or sibling standing over them with hands on hips declaring, "Who are you to think you can become something great?" We are all capable of anything we dream into being! When we treat ourselves with kindness, eliminating the self-limiting and destructive dialogue that can sometimes become an insidious pattern, our life begins to shift. Self-love replaces self-loathing. The internal conversation morphs into one of, "Who am I to believe I *can't* accomplish something great?" Exploration into new possibilities begins. When we treat ourselves lovingly, believe we are worth the best care, the best treatment, the best circumstances, over time we begin to believe it with all of our heart. We start to expect that our life mirrors this worth. If we're treated poorly, become weary of lack or we begin to recognize boredom or stagnancy, a little voice begins to form, which gets louder and louder if ignored, a little voice that declares, "I deserve and desire more. I choose a new experience."

Self-love also creates room for occasional failures. Seth Godin, American business entrepreneur and bestselling author, writes about failure in his book, *Poke the Box*, "There will be other jobs, better jobs, bosses more willing to create growth. The only way you will find those jobs and those bosses, though, is to have a personal standard that demands failure, not one that guarantees success. Intellectual integrity goes beyond being clever—it requires that you put your ideas into the world." Self-love fosters the ability to remain fearless, creative and innovative in all of our endeavors. Nearly all of the great innovators in our history have welcomed failure as a steppingstone to wholeness. Isn't this a testament to self-love?

Benjamin Zander, world-class conductor for the Boston Philharmonic Orchestra and co-author of the book, *The Art of Possibility*, has written one of my favorite passages on the celebration of failure. He writes, "It is dangerous to have our musicians so obsessed with competition because they will find it difficult to take the necessary risks with themselves to be great performers. The art of music, since it can only be conveyed through its interpreters, depends on the expressive performance for its lifeblood. Yet it is only when we make mistakes in performance that we can really begin to notice what needs attention. In fact, I actively train my students that when they make a mistake, they are to lift their arms in the air, smile and say, 'How fascinating!' I recommend that everyone try this."

What would happen if the next time you made a perceived mistake (remember with S.T.A.R. all is perfect) that instead of treating yourself cruelly you would instead declare, "How fascinating!" and simply review the events from the point of view of the Fascinated Observer, noticing the facts without the distortion of judgment and criticism. Mistakes are simply steppingstones to growth and expansion. They are opportunities for refinement.

> FIND FASCINATION WITH EVERY EXPERIENCE.

Activity: Observe/Snap/Re-vision

Take a moment to think about a recent event that triggered an unwanted emotional response. Perhaps you've associated that event with the concept of a mistake or a failure. When you remember that event, can you feel yourself contract, your energy field getting smaller, simply as a result of remembering? Hold on to that for a moment so you can re-vision the event with fascination.

What did you learn from it?

Love yourself for learning it.

Did it benefit you in some way, by making you stronger perhaps or wiser?

Love yourself for observing the benefits.

Observe how you responded.

Love yourself for responding in that manner.

Once you have observed, now reflect—what do you find fascinating about this situation?

Express gratitude for the wisdom you gained from that situation.

The next time you find yourself getting triggered into this place of quantum contraction:

1. *Observe* what is happening.

2. *Snap* out of it and into fascination for the event.

3. *Re-vision* the experience into something you can use to progress your life onward.

Make these three simple steps a practice throughout your day. You may journal your experiences or share them with a S.T.A.R. study group of your choosing. *Trust* that the more often we can retrain our consciousness to transcend our fears and lack of *Self-love*, the faster our baseline perception expands into the place where all things are possible.

FUN WITH FAILURE

My (Kristy's) client, John, had agreed to take on a film project that was way outside his comfort zone. He was thrilled beyond measure and also a little afraid. He had never done something of this scope before and his primitive lizard brain was acting out. "You can't do this! You've never done this before! What if you (gasp) FAIL?" were his rampaging thoughts. Why? Because our survival mechanisms are never a big fan of failure. When the possibility exists, that's when we generally make unconscious moves to keep us small, stagnant and safe. Anything is better to our pride and sensibility than the concept of falling flat on our face. Knowing what was taking place within his being—there was a subpersonality within him not happy about taking this bold step—he used Observe/Snap/Re-vision!

Knowing the importance of failure in the course of history, knowing how many world-altering innovations the bricks of failure have paved, he decided to shift this fear into the energy of fun. Together we created the mantra, "Let's fail at this!" Every time he said it out loud, his fist pumping in enthusiastic support, we couldn't help but laugh. He revised his entire perception! The truth is there is no such thing as failure if you can observe into its essence, which is that every misstep is a tremendous learning experience which pushes our growth edge and brings to us a larger foundation from which to work. His mantra, "Let's fail at this!" allowed him to stop taking himself so seriously. He laughed; he lightened up. It allowed his energy to shift so he could get out of his own way and work the project, which was ultimately great fun and a tremendous growth experience.

Observe: John observed what was taking place and recognized that his fear was getting in the way of his soul's desire for growth. He would not have felt whole had he dropped out of this project.

Snap: He snapped into a new way of perceiving by connecting to the essential quality of *Self-love*. He knew that he was capable of handling this new work project, which pushed his growth edge.

Re-vision: His perception of "failure" was revised into that of a potential rite of passage; something one chooses to risk on the pathway to soul expression. This allowed him the expansiveness needed to *Surrender* to his fear, *Trust* in himself, *Allow* for the project and *Receive* joy, gratitude, experience, confidence and prosperity as a result of his success.

COMMITMENT TO PLAY

Commitment to *Play (the now moment)* is essential not only to our spiritual, physical and mental health, but is crucial to remaining in a creative and innovative space. When we play, we enter a vortex of timelessness. We may even glance up at the clock and four hours have disappeared without us noticing. That's what it feels like when work + play + fascination is activated. This is where we tap into the Universal current of divine manifestation. In this space, this moment, where we forget about what we haven't accomplished in the past or the worries of some fictional future, we plug into our own immortality, where time has no meaning.

I (Kristy) once devoted an entire month to working with people who normally couldn't afford my coaching rates. I did it as a pay-it-forward because my own mentor offered to work with me for a rate I could afford, far below what he normally charged. I had also identified a little voice inside of me deep within my consciousness which whispered, "Nobody can afford coaching." So I blasted it with the energy of *Play* (*the now moment*). I made it fun and I advertised that for this particular month, I was working with anyone who wanted coaching, for whatever they could afford. A huge number of people responded, inviting me to wonder with fascination if I had done the right thing! Was I out of my mind? How was I going to work with this number of people?! What had I done? And then a miracle happened. I began working with this incredible group, one by one, listening to their stories, their dreams, their visions for manifesting their perfect life and the concept of time and money fell away entirely. I realized that a packed schedule—doing this thing that I loved—didn't bother me and I realized that if someone paid me $10 for an hour I loved the process as much as if somebody paid me $200 an hour. What a revelation! And through it, I connected to all three forms of richness:

Material—I was earning money from twenty-four new clients.

Spiritual—I suddenly had a full schedule doing my soul's work.

Relational—I was connecting on a divine level with all of these amazing new people in my life.

This experience taught me that my work was play. When I made that connection, the unfortunately prophetic voice which had previously whispered, "Nobody can afford coaching," also fell away, becoming entirely irrelevant. I proved it wrong. This allowed me to create a new reality, one where people could afford coaching. For me, these twenty-four new clients had become my definition of richness, setting a new foundation for my own prosperity. Once I had connected to that divine current, I knew the money would continue to flow, as long as I didn't limit it with my own narrow perceptions by focusing on what people could not afford, creating the very reality I was trying to avoid. *Play (the now moment)* saved the day!

Think about when you earned your first dollar. Not your first paycheck from your first job, we mean your first dollar, literally. How old were you? Five or six? What did you do to earn it? Think back to recall this experience. Do you remember the joy and fascination you felt with that crisp bill clenched in your sweaty little hand? Now think about this moment in time. How do you earn your money? Can you find a connection between the joy you felt earning this first dollar bill and the work you do today?

Activity: Viewing Richness with the Eyes of a Child

How can we observe money through the eyes of a child and bring the joy of childhood into our wallets? When we have deep affection and appreciation for even the smallest level of prosperity we shift into an expansive octave that allows for more to come.

Let's play! You will need paper money, a few coins and a debit or credit card.

Hold each type of money in your hand, separately.

◎ What happens in your body when you feel the soft malleability of the paper money, the jingle of the metal coins, the razor edge of the plastic card?

◎ Watch with fascination as any deeply embedded beliefs about money come rising to the surface with this exercise, perhaps appearing as nothing more than somatic sensations.

◎ Are there thoughts? Feelings? Perhaps a simple body awareness such as an opening of your throat or a tightness in your chest or a clenching of your stomach? Do you become softer or more rigid in their presence? We're only observing here, not judging.

Sit with those sensations for a moment. Now hold all three (coins, paper money and the debit card).

◎ Which of the three is easiest to receive for you?

◎ Which has a positive charge for you?

◎ Do you feel lighter when you hold one or all?

◎ Do any carry a negative charge?

Building a New Sandcastle

I (Nina) had searched all of my coat pockets imagining that there would be enough coins in them collectively to put in the pay phone at the gas station, which was about a mile from my apartment in Santa Fe. My phone had been disconnected, my lease was being terminated and I felt alone. I needed to reach out to my children to let them know that I was OK.

As I held the coins, I had a deep knowing that the value they represented did not reflect my inner value. The condition in which I found myself was not who I was. I knew that my life would magically change. The how was unknown.

As I wrote in my book, *Return of Love to Planet Earth, Memoir of a Reluctant Visionary*, what this experience gifted me with was a profound realization that God was not outside of me, but inside of me. It was as if I had to lose everything that no longer served me in order to rebuild my personal identity within a new framework of being a divine human.

Subconsciously, I had created a situation that was life changing, which many would have judged as failure. What I see now, as the Fascinated Observer, is that those few coins in my hand were gifting me wealth and abundance that transcended their perceived monetary worth. Like sand through my fingers, those coins represented nothing more than building blocks. They had the fragile stability of the structure of a sandcastle—a new reality—I could continue to create or kick apart, smooth out the sand and rebuild in any moment. Beautiful!

○ Do they make you feel compressed inside, uncomfortable?

○ Let's say that each form of currency has its own spirit. If they did, what would they convey to you about your relationship with them?

○ When you are communicating about money, what are you saying most frequently? What is the energy of your words? What happens within your body?

○ If you had to distill this experience into one sentence which summarized your internal beliefs surrounding money—a belief that is ready to shift into something new, something without fear or discomfort—what would that be?

Now, on a blank piece of paper, choose to write about the internal limiting belief system surrounding money that you are ready to transform.

RE-VISIONING OUR MONEY FOUNDATION

What if we learned to re-vision our beliefs about money into this simple concept: *We build our own belief systems around money.* What if we brought into this new knowing of ours a sense of the Four Essential Qualities? We are individual expressions of All That Is, our *Wholeness (human divinity)* wants for nothing. We embody *Self-love* by believing in our divine human expression and allowing for new possibilities surrounding money. We live in the *Play (the now moment)*, each experience a tool in our capacity for building. And the *Embodiment of the Expanded Golden Rule* broadens the scope of our financial beliefs to include caring for Mother Earth, our fellow humans and every sentient being on our planet.

Note what starts to shift as your belief systems learn to re-vision? Think about the entire world undergoing the same re-visioning exercise and feel it in your body as though a global transformation surrounding money has already taken place. A new paradigm based on the understanding that money is an exchange of divine love energy and nothing more. What if...?! Nothing to fear, nothing to fight over, just the currency of the heart. When we think of it in this light, isn't it a supreme gift to get to pay the electric bill, for example? There are those in our world who don't have that option. And how can we possibly complain about the water bill, knowing of those who struggle with finding enough? When we decide to go to a nice restaurant to eat, it doesn't serve us to fret over the check; we're supporting the livelihood of all who work there. In turn we are open to receiving those who wish to patronize our business.

A friend of mine (Kristy's) was having an issue with her husband. Living in Santa Fe, she loved to amble around the plaza and the artist's mecca of Canyon Road, enjoying the world-class art for its pure beauty. He, by contrast, would continually pull her along, not allowing her to partake in this joy, for fear that she would want to buy something! "We can't afford that!" he'd bark. "It's $54,000!" he'd point to the price tag as she stopped to relish a sculpture. It was so disheartening to her, not having any intention of purchasing these things! To be constantly reminded of what she could not afford was becoming a real drag. Loving her husband immensely and knowing that his anxiety was based on a deep fear of "never having enough" she introduced him to the philosophy of S.T.A.R., and a metamorphosis took place. Truly wanting to shift this pattern, over time he learned to:

○ *Surrender* to the knowing that he was feeling fearful and powerless around money.

○ *Trust* that he could create a new reality, committing to his desire to transform this fear energy into something new.

○ *Allow* for something new to form, though he had no idea what that would look like at the time.

○ *Receive* a new sense of peace and freedom around the entire concept of abundance and prosperity.

They now have a new fun exercise to imprint the understanding that there is more to richness than material wealth. When they walk around Canyon Road today, she points out everything she knows he loves. She stops at the $30,000 painting and she says, "I'm going to buy this for you, honey." And he says, "Thank you, Baby! I wonder where I'll hang it?" They wink and move on, knowing it's not about having the resources to spend thousands of dollars on art. It's about remaining open to any possibility and simply enjoying the richness of the moment together.

Now, take a moment to re-vision your beliefs around money. Review your internal limiting belief system that you are ready to transform (page 57). After considering the examples below, write a personal power statement or mantra to assist this shift. You may also choose to pick an image; such as every time you see the form of a butterfly, you can sense your re-visioning taking place.

Some examples of personal power statements (mantras) are:

I always have enough

I always have what I need

I always have an abundance

Now you try it. Complete this statement from a personal point of view:

"The mantra or image I have chosen to help shift my internal limiting belief system surrounding money is:"

Take a moment to bring in all of your Four Essential Qualities—*Wholeness (human divinity), Self-love, Play (the now moment)* and the *Embodiment of the Expanded Golden Rule.* Write a paragraph in the space below which explains how you will bring all of these qualities into the re-vision you will create within your own life, to shift into a new way of being with the energy of money.

If you feel open to it, please share your paragraph with anyone you feel will support you in making this shift. Saying it out loud, sharing it with others, serves as a declaration, which builds energy and support from all realms to assist you.

QUANTUM FIELD TRIP

Remember the joy you felt the first time you got to take a field trip with your school? It was a full day out of the classroom, engaging with life in an entirely new way! I (Kristy) remember mine like it was yesterday. I was seven years old, and on the last day of school we piled in a bus and drove a hundred miles to visit the Denver Mint. I was exhilarated beyond measure! Wide eyed and fascinated, I watched as all the coins shot around the enormous expanse of that place, silicone tubes filled with rapids of cascading silver. It was loud and it was glorious. My parents had given me five dollars to spend as I saw fit and how abundantly rich I felt! I found something in the gift shop that completely delighted me. Spending a nickel of my five dollar bounty, I purchased a tiny glass bottle with a minuscule cork. Inside was a penny. "How did it get inside?" I marveled with incredulity, not having any experience with the magic of glass-blowing. After a full day in Denver, exhausted and spent like my five-dollar bill, we piled back into the bus and returned to our tiny town, where life was much less grandiose. When I arrived home, I showed my family my treasure—the tiny bottle with the penny inside. My older brother, unimpressed, hardly looked up from his comic book and joked, "You spent a nickel for a penny! Smart." He clearly didn't get it! This was magic!

> CAN YOU ACCEPT THAT THE BALANCE IN YOUR "COSMIC" BANK ACCOUNT IS INFINITE?

My enthusiasm for that coin in the bottle is undiminished—I still see it as valuable and I still have the little corked bottle today. The penny rests inside sitting on my altar, reminding me of what the pure sensation of abundance feels like. If I made a million dollars tomorrow, it wouldn't surpass the richness I felt that day, as a child at the Denver Mint, with five dollars in my hand and an open door to possibility.

I clearly remember that experience and now understand that my financial belief systems at that age were unformed. On that field trip, the massive amount of money I saw at the Denver Mint was simply awe-inspiring. It was beautiful, nothing more and much like the natural wonders I had the fortune of exploring around my glorious home state of Colorado.

The energy of richness was so potent for me that day that it still powers me decades later, all the magic of the Denver Mint corked in my minuscule glass bottle, broadcasting across all time and space from its present-day location on my alter. The abundance isn't connected to financial value—I suppose even if the precious thing has doubled in value these thirty-five years later I could trade a dime for it today; for me the sentimental value is so much deeper than the tangible. Holding it in my hand is an open door that never closes for me, the Denver Mint's energy churning within, reminding me that whatever I choose to manifest is within my divine grasp.

Do you have a similar story? Something you call on to remind yourself of what abundance means for you? How about creating a brand new story!

Activity: Take Your Own Quantum Field Trip

Choose a business, institution or place to visit and do so with the intention of igniting your imagination into a brand new place of Universal richness. Take this field trip with your friends, family or by yourself. Do this trip with the intention of shifting octaves by challenging your firmly established belief systems.

Some examples include:

Go to any fine jewelry establishment. Focus on the simple beauty of the diamonds. Don't allow your triggers, beliefs or the million-dollar price tags to snag you. Simply connect with the energy of the diamonds. See what diamonds have to teach you.

1. Do you feel you "belong" in the store? Are these stones worth the dollar sign attached to them?

2. Who decides their worth?

3. Are they alive?

4. Witness your body sensations as you peruse the cases with the eyes of the Fascinated Observer.

Visit a major art museum. Take in the creativity without thinking of the value. Imagine you could simply take a painting off the wall—the Mona Lisa if you choose—and take it home with you.

1. Where would you hang it?

2. What would you feel every time you studied it, hanging there above your fireplace?

3. What if it had no financial value?

4. Would you still cherish it?

Take a hike in nature. Contemplate all of the creatures who live within it, the birds, the animals, the insects, the flowers, the trees, the rocks and soil.

1. Does their life appear to be rich? Imagine your love, or lack of love for this environment feeding it, contributing to its richness or its scarcity.

2. Find a place to rest and choose a being with whom to "speak." Perhaps you see a curious bird watching you or a friendly tree shading you or an insect resting on a rock. Choose the being and ask it what it has to teach you about what abundance means to it? Accept anything you hear as truth, even if you feel you're "making it up."

3. How does this conversation affect your own feelings of abundance? What happens within you as you open to this possibility?

4. Thank the being with whom you've spoken by offering a token of gratitude. Leave a pinch of tobacco, sage or lavender or create a tiny pool of water in a rock groove from your own drinking supply. Dedicate this offering to the entire forest for having welcomed you into its sacred space.

Go to a fast food restaurant.

1. What do you believe about fast food?

2. Is it a blessing or a curse?

3. Regardless of your beliefs, leave any judgments at the door. Just observe for this exercise. Enter as though you've never seen a place like this before; as though you're just discovering the concept of fast food for the first time.

4. Consider all that are employed within its reach; imagine that the corporation cares deeply for its managers and the managers in turn care deeply for all those employed by them.

5. Consider that this establishment is serving a divine role that you might not be able to fully assess, know that all is perfect. What could this divine role be? What if they are a catalyst for shifting the world into expanded octaves?

6. What if it takes what that restaurant is doing in the world to bring about change, perhaps to illuminate how we can do things differently?

7. What do you see happening that *is* aligned with the Four Essential Qualities of *Wholeness (human divinity), Self-love, Play (the now moment)* and the *Embodiment of the Expanded Golden Rule*? Imagine all that does not align with these qualities falling away, being de-created to make space for the new world that you are creating.

Wherever you go, whatever perfect choice you make, take your quantum field trip with gratitude and an open mind. Have the intention to open your energy field into the appropriate octave for you.

Did the experience inspire you to think bigger or give you an "Ah-ha!" moment?

Did it trigger new desires in your own life?

Did your perceptions change?

What was the most fascinating thing?

What did you observe that you had not noticed before?

THE RICHES OF INTERCONNECTEDNESS

The *Expanded Golden Rule* is the last Essential Quality of S.T.A.R. "Do unto all of creation as I would have all of creation do unto me." In other words, every being across the globe, all forms of sentient life, all energy forms and earthly creations—including so-called inanimate objects—should be treated with love, dignity and respect. If not, we cannot expect to receive love, dignity and respect for ourselves. Interconnection dictates that if we harm another, we harm ourselves and vice versa.

All work, including that which comes with no paycheck, if approached with integrity and soul, leads to beauty. All work is sacred. Philip Zaleski and Paul Kaufman, in their book, *Gifts of the Spirit*, write that "work is a superb ascetic discipline, a tonic that nourishes just those qualities—endurance, courage, concentration—that support inner life." But, is our life's work making the world stronger or at least not weakening it? It's a fascinating question.

Contemplating how the wisdom of this expanded rule applies to prosperity, work and abundance, we are reminded how many dolphins die in monofilament and crab trap lines. Then my mind travels to the fish kills that are reported often from pesticides seeping into major bodies of water or oil from drilling rigs. What seems evident is that the individual or corporate short-sighted pursuits of prosperity and abundance through work efforts have not taken into consideration "all of creation."

The long-term return from this myopic view is loss of pure water, death of species and contamination of soil. The *Expanded Golden Rule* puts us in balance with all forms of creation, not just human with human, as the Golden Rule suggests. Mother Earth provides abundance naturally. We are prosperous when we respect that balance. Pods of dolphin will flourish, schools of fish will provide nourishment and healthy soil will sustain our crops well into the future. Living the *Embodiment of the Expanded Golden Rule* states that we honor and love all of creation.

Right Livelihood is one aspect of the *Embodiment of the Expanded Golden Rule*, a Buddhist concept which states that what we do for a living should bring no harm to ourselves or others. Thich Nhat Hanh, in his book, *The Heart of the Buddha's Teaching*, says this about it: "To practice Right Livelihood (samyagajiva) you find a way to earn your living without transgressing your ideals of love and compassion. The way you support yourself can be an expression of your deepest self or it can be a source of suffering for you and others."

Quantum physics tells us that we are all One Consciousness made up of waves of possibility, not atoms that are solid. If this is the case, the concept of Right Livelihood seems a powerful one. If our behaviors cause us suffering in or outside the confines of our daily work, we are likely experiencing incongruence between how we're showing up in the world and what it is that our divine self chose to experience in this incarnation. Are perceived societal expectations getting in the way of your heart path? If so, ask yourself if your perceived societal

Expanding the Golden Rule

In 2008, I (Nina) had an opportunity to go to the Clearwater Marine Aquarium to visit Winter, of the movie, *Dolphin Tale* fame. Winter's story is that when she was three months old she was trapped in a crab trap line and was unable to escape. Winter was rescued and taken to the Clearwater Marine Aquarium where her tail and two vertebrae were removed. While I was watching her swim in her tank, the *Embodiment of the Expanded Golden Rule* came to me: *Do unto all creation what you would have all of creation do unto you.*

expectations are simply an illusion your survival mechanisms have constructed to keep you small. It's never easy to step away from the safety of the crowd, but the truth is millions have done it and just as many are revered as ridiculed. The *Expanded Golden Rule* asks that we understand that the entire universe is working to support the desires of our heart and soul.

Rasha writes in the channeled book, *Oneness*, "The question is not what one chooses to be doing, so much as the intent with which one chooses to be doing it. When one is focused upon material gain as an end in itself, the outcome is constricted by the foundation of fear upon which scarcity is based. When one is focused upon selfless service to the higher good of All Life, without fear for one's own wellbeing, the highest result is manifested for all." What if abundance isn't what your mind tells you it is? In fact, what if it looks completely different? What if the true definition of prosperity is simply a rich experience, a balance between material, spiritual and relational wealth? Does this open up a whole new world of possibility? What about those who want to win the lottery so they can buy their mother a house, their best friend a luxury car, their spouse or partner a voyage around the world? Prosperity to some means the ability to give it to others!

Think of how many rich experiences we collect through our interconnections with the world around us. Interacting with a kind stranger, a friendly butterfly or a ripe apple tree offering the abundance of her glorious September fruit. If we accepted these as cosmic paychecks we'd be making deposits beyond our wildest dreams, wouldn't we? Perhaps gratitude is the true currency. The *Expanded Golden Rule* is about all of creation working together to create perfection in our lives in relation to prosperity. This perfection is created through the experiences and situations we co-create in each moment.

FINDING THE SOURCE

When we can observe with fascination where our belief systems and responses originate and get in the way of our ability as divine humans to creatively express, we take quantum leaps. Our perceptions about possibilities can instantly expand. Following those leaps, we know where to place our focus and use the richness of our gifts to create new ways to be on earth. Remember that when fascination is applied to prosperity, we can dream into being ALL that we need to support us in achieving that which we came to earth to accomplish. We hope you have accepted the invitation to first understand what prosperity means to you, which may have nothing to do with work or money.

Embodying our divine understanding of abundance may be served by observing how we're being, snapping our intention to a new way of seeing, to re-vision a brand new story upon which to build. It may mean calling on the energy of childhood whimsy and play if we become stuck.

PART TWO:
FASCINATED BY RELATIONSHIPS

Willingly Taking Direction from Our Own Divine Self—A New Level of Confidence

From *S.T.A.R. Philosophy* by Nina Brown (page 125)

We have spent years following the spiritual direction of others, looking outside of ourselves for guidance in matters of the spirit. The idea that our divine wisdom lies within is new for many and for me as well. How can we trust this remembering? It is indeed a remembering, for there was a time when we knew this to be true. I believe that during the Golden Age of Lemuria and the Golden Age of Atlantis we knew our divinity. Then we forgot. How do we return to a sovereign state of being? The personality tries to block us by screaming "Pride! Arrogance! Be humble? Not you!" Yet within, there is a yearning to surrender, trust and allow this possibility to expand and to then receive fully the love of you for YOU.

As we open this door of a new reality and walk in as the master that we are, the devil and the angel sitting on our shoulders will be trying to get our attention. One way to merge the polarities tugging at us in opposite directions and to achieve self-realization is by means of community. Seek with intention those beings of light on the planet who radiate the harmonics of the divine Creator. Sit by their side. Listen to their words and entrain with their frequency. You will unlock the veiled memory of your truth and, with each clear breath of life filling your Being, will awaken to the knowing in every cell, that you are a divine human. The community of sovereign beings will support you in transitioning to your wholeness until you can stand tall and be a model for others.

CHAPTER THREE:
KNOWING ME

HAVE YOU EVER SAID OR FELT THE WORDS, "I'm not sure I know who I am"? A taste of this unknowing brings a profound sense of loss and sorrow so deep, we can begin to question the meaning of everything around us. When we lose our anchor to our own Wholeness (human divinity), our sense of belonging or place in the world disappears. It's possible to grieve the loss of self. This place of dark unknowingness can feel unbearably painful. How do we find our connection once again or perhaps for the first time? It's a question we could ask entire cultures; indeed entire societies can become collectively lost. The question we invite you to contemplate is: do I want my old familiar connection or am I ready to revise the octave at which I connect to my divinity? To revise our connection, we can begin with that question.

Some people postulate that we've all heard that the industrialized world is becoming more and more lonely as people become nomadic, frequently moving to the next great opportunity, consistently breaking community ties. It's not unusual for the average American to claim one or two good friends in their life, many times connecting only with those at work without forming any lasting, deep relationships outside of their immediate family. But if we're not staying true to our relationships with our community, a variety of unpleasing states of being may arise, including loneliness. We have to build a strong connection of self-love before we can develop strong connections externally, otherwise looking outside of self to find fulfillment becomes an unending quest. Looking outside of ourselves means we say things like:

○ I live in Timbuktu and can't possibly find anyone to relate to here.

○ I've opened myself up to people in the past and I always get screwed, so never again.

○ Nobody *gets me* so why even try?

○ No more decent single men (or women) are left in the world.

○ Nobody really wants to hang out with me.

○ There's no time in my life for friendships. It's all I can do to keep up with the demands of my family.

We are nourished by each other. And as long as we stay true to ourselves and our individual needs (it's true that some people need more connection than others), we lay the foundation for finding our own connection. Discovering peace and harmony in our relationships, communities and connections begins with finding harmony within ourselves. John O'Donohue wrote in *Anam Cara*, "In each person, there is a point of absolute nonconnection with everything else and with everyone. This is fascinating and frightening. It means that we cannot continue to seek outside ourselves for the things we need from within. The blessings for which we hunger are not to be found in other places or people. These gifts can only be given to you by yourself. They are at home at the hearth of your soul."

The micro impacts the macro. The Heavens impact us, so do we impact the Heavens and all relationships begin with developing right relationship with ourselves. David Abram in his book *The Spell of the Sensuous* speaks of harmony, which for the Navajo is the word *hozho*. He writes, "When a Navajo person wishes to renew or reestablish, in the world, the harmonious condition of wellbeing and beauty expressed by the Navajo word *hozho* he must first strive, through ritual, to create this harmony and peacefulness within his own being. Having established such *hozho* within himself, he can then actively impart this state of wellbeing to the enveloping cosmos, through the transforming power of song or prayer." What does it mean for us to choose a harmonious condition of wellbeing in our life? It may start with self-care.

What happens in your body when you speak the statement: "Nothing matters but me." You may have experienced a host of conflicting feelings. Was there a reflex within you that protested the "selfishness" of that statement? We've all heard the pre-flight lectures about putting the oxygen mask on ourselves before our children. This seems logical, right? I mean, how can we assist our children if we allow ourselves to become hypoxic and drop over? And yet, in some cultures there can be collective resistance around the concept that putting ourselves first is imperative to our daily survival. What if we took the concept of "guilt" and threw it out the window? If we do that, we may find that the statement, "Nothing matters but me," frees us from an awful lot of burdens, for example, trying to control others. "But I can do it so much better!" we tell ourselves, "They're ruining their life! I have no choice but to intervene, take charge." Allowing somebody else their own sovereignty, recognizing them as a divine being making their own choices and navigating their own struggles is the greatest gift we can give to another. It means we put our trust and faith in their sovereign choices. That doesn't mean we withhold our love. Oftentimes a person struggling with their life can be so buoyed by the love we give them that the connection itself is enough to spark them into making new choices, having a greater sense of empowerment and control over their own life. What happens when we elbow our presence into their choices and decisions, letting them know that we're here to rescue them? Not exactly empowering.

Activity: A Question of Control

Who have you longed to control in your life? Is it an adult child who just can't seem to figure out how to navigate the world as you would? Is it a parent who drinks too much? How about a friend who continually chooses destructive relationships and then makes a habit of calling you sobbing at 2:00 in the morning? Take a moment to connect with this fascinating relationship. You may tell yourself a story that this person's life is out of control. What effect is this story having on *your* life? Take some time to answer the following questions:

- What insight am I being asked to *Surrender* in this relationship?

- What do I already know but am avoiding?

- What would it take for me to let go and *Trust* that this person, as much as I love them, has their own sacred journey to navigate?

- What if stepping away from their drama, choosing not to enmesh myself in the events of their life, could *Allow* them to own their own divinity?

- What if my interference is robbing them of the critical insight that would help them see their own divinity?

◉ What would stepping away from the drama look like to me and how does it feel in my body to visualize already having done it?

◉ What do I wish to *Receive* from freeing myself from the entanglement of somebody else's choices? How will my life change when I make the choice to do so?

Take as much time as you need to contemplate these questions from your wholeness.

Consider navigating this experience with a community of friends and sharing your answers with one another. If it's a small enough gathering, breaking into groups may not be necessary. Allow everyone ample time to express themselves and offer only sacred listening with an open heart and mind, speaking or communicating with no judgment or advice! This isn't about solving another person's problem; it's about detaching from our instincts to do so.

AWARENESS OF PERSONAL FIXATIONS

I (Kristy) had an incredible and life-changing dream a few years ago. I was stuck in a pattern of intense pain over the suffering animals of the world. It was what I chose to fixate on at the time, likely stemming from twenty years of working in veterinary medicine. I hadn't processed much of the pain I experienced in my career—more cases of profound suffering than I could handle—and after I left the field I fell into a path of trying to rescue every feral cat and dog in the rough little mountain town of Raton, New Mexico, where I had recently moved from the relatively tidy and pristine existence I had in Minneapolis, Minnesota.

There were animals who suffered there, but I couldn't *see them* everyday all around me like I had the privilege of experiencing in New Mexico. They wandered the streets, they showed up on my porch. I was clearly broadcasting a flashing Universal neon sign that read, "Every suffering animal in the state, kindly show up on my door step! My heart's not broken enough as it is." I was going crazy with grief.

DOES EMPOWERMENT IMPLY THAT WE POSSESS THE WISDOM TO CURE SELF?

So one night, I received incredible insight into this pattern that I was meant to transcend in the form of a dream. In this dream, the night was inky black with a full illuminated moon casting its light across an urban yard, beautifully tended. I was inside, with a screenless window wide open, sitting on the polished hardwood floor, gazing out into the darkness. I couldn't sleep. Arms folded on the open windowpane, I rested my chin on my wrists, enjoying the night breeze when from the dark depths of the yard wandered a Pomeranian dog. "How sweet!" I thought, becoming alert, holding my breath. "What's she doing out there?" I wondered. Preparing to spring into action to scoop her up out of the darkness, a fox pounced out of the brush and grabbed her in her mouth. "Oh God! No!" I screamed and then a tiny litter of baby kits (little foxes) followed behind her. I froze. All those tiny adorable babies with tummies rumbling, hungry…I felt their joy. So confused, I lost my ability to think. If I saved the Pomeranian, how would the tiny fox babies fare? Just then, a coyote leaped out of the bushes, rushing the mama fox. "No!" I shrieked! And just as before, a litter of coyote pups rolled out of the bush cheerfully following their mama, their only concern their growling bellies. "What do I do? Who do I save?" I melted down, adrenaline pounding. I leaned out the window, my instinct to save somebody too powerful and at that moment an enormous Mountain Lion leaped out of the darkness directly at my face. Without thinking, I shot back into the house, quickly slamming the windowpane down, my heart nearly bursting. A deep male voice then answered my question, "*Who do you save? You save yourself.*" And I woke up out of the dream, my heart racing. I understood that this was the only option. In my life, it was a call to action. If I tended to my own wounds, I would be much better equipped to do the big work I desired to do in this world. It wasn't about giving in and never again reaching out my hand to those in need. It was about understanding that working to save every being in the world *but myself*, was not helping anyone.

Activity: Dream Messengers

What if we considered our dreams to be messages from distant realms? Or perhaps we could believe they are communications from deep within the vast landscape inside of us? What feels right to you?

Recall a dream you've had that has altered the course of your life or perhaps simply inspired great insight within you. These dreams don't have to come in the boundaries of the container of a story line; they can simply be fragments of images or emotion that have a profound effect on you. Waking with a deep sense of emotion, dreams like this stick with us throughout the day or perhaps weeks or months into our future.

If you've had several of these, which one is vying for your attention in this moment? Take a moment to connect with it, thanking whatever force you believe delivered it to you; perhaps it was handed down from your own divinity or perhaps you feel it was a direct transmission from another being asking to connect with you. Whatever its source, open to it with gratitude, accepting the gift in whatever form it arrives. Dreams can be profound guides in our life, if we allow their messages to permeate us. They are an unlimited transformational spiritual resource for us. Be sure to offer great gratitude when you receive it, to whomever you feel has delivered this gift. If you normally have no memory of your dreams, set the intention to do so and then be open to receiving whatever comes. Maybe it's just a feeling or a sense of expansion. Regardless, accept that it's all perfect.

Do this with the intention of receiving another sacred message in dream form over the next seventy-two hours. Ask a specific question, such as "Reveal to me my divine path in this moment" and allow the reception of the dream, contemplating it each night before you go to sleep.

My Priorities

By saying, "Nothing matters but me" or "We save ourselves first," we are in essence saying, "My priority is that I observe my own life first." It's saying that in this moment I choose to focus on myself. That means that anyone else can make any other choice they aspire to as a divine, sovereign being and that choice is perfect. I am free to find fascination in their choices. For the sake of experience, it may be our choice to be the servant of another, but we are not anyone else's Lord. We are all sacred beings having an earthly experience for the sake of expansion and growth. The Fascinated Observer understands this and is not drawn into old paradigm thoughts such as judging others for the choices they make. We lose the need to exert control over another so-called "weaker" being, because in reality there is no such thing. We learn that we are all spiritual equals, and we learn that our ability to love others depends on our own embodiment of self-love.

Save yourself. Focus on yourself. A man I (Kristy) greatly admire, best-selling author, anthropologist and shamanic healer, Alberto Villoldo, told me that sorcery is setting the intention to alter another person's life. No matter if we believe that intention is in their "best interest." Interference is not honoring, unless they've invited it. We are not here to judge another's experience. We're here to navigate our own and love those around us to the best of our abilities.

CHAPTER FOUR:
OUR RELATIONSHIPS WITH OTHERS

Beyond Compassion

Adapted from *S.T.A.R. Philosophy* by Nina Brown (page 145)

When we are in divine relationship with others we can:

Surrender the will to consistently advise.

Trust that every being is purely expressing their own octave of divinity in a manner that is perfect.

Allow the people we interact with to transcend without judging where they are on their path.

Receive liberation from believing we have a responsibility to heal the world and recognize that our only assignment is to love the world.

MOVING BEYOND COMPASSION IS FASCINATING. The founder of the Omega Institute and author of *The Seeker's Guide*, Elizabeth Lesser, weighs in on this subject when she writes, "Your self-knowledge and self-love are the most unselfish gifts you can give to another. Self-knowledge makes you clear, strong and trustworthy and allows others to know where you stand. Self-love makes love of others more genuine." She goes on to quote Indian poet Rabindranath Tagore who writes, "He who wants to do good knocks at the gate; he who loves finds the gate open."

Bringing the Four Essential Qualities into this understanding looks something like this:

Wholeness (human divinity)—We are divine beings who orchestrate our experience. In accepting this, we understand that others are also perfect, complete and whole on their own path to wholeness. We can choose our own path, but we can't choose another's. We allow them their divinity and the freedom to choose.

Self-love—We understand that we are a reflection of the divine and the divine is a reflection of us. To create love-centered change in the world, we need only start with ourselves. Learning to embody self-love brings love to all beings, which then returns to us.

Play (the now moment)—Understanding that only this moment is truth allows us to let go of the need for controlling the outcome or destiny of anything outside of ourselves. Our judgments of others, need for control and anxiety over the path of another have a foundation in fear, sadness and distrust. When we align with our own timelessness, the power of the moment and connect with our frequency of joy, we bring healing to our self which in turn radiates through all of creation.

Embodiment of the Expanded Golden Rule—Just as we accept our own divinity, we understand that we are all divinely choosing our own unique experiences throughout this lifetime. This means that it is not up to us to "save" every creature on the planet from its suffering (which we know to be an impossible endeavor anyway). Every creature is creating his own unique spiritual experience, manifesting her own divine path through every experience. We are not superior to each other, nor are we superior to the animals and the trees and the insects. We are here, custodians of this new earth in harmony with all beings. We learn from each other.

FIRST ENCOUNTERS: THE FAMILIES WE GROW WITH

People can despise their family, avoid their family, consider their family the greatest gift in their life, be completely indifferent or be obsessed with their family. We run the gamut with family experiences from completely detaching to becoming so enmeshed we don't know where they end and we begin. I've heard a lot of psychologists say, "I can be sane with anyone except my family members!" Our histories are so deep and extensive it becomes supremely difficult to become the Fascinated Observer when we're at Thanksgiving dinner or the annual family reunion. All of our relationships are an instrument from the collective Universal field. We can start to believe that when we understand that nobody can do anything to us. We can choose not to identify with the victim title.

No matter what bliss or grief we are offered, the experiences we are living in relation to the family we grew up with are a sacred gift. That's not to say they aren't also painful as hell. Not everybody has good memories of their life, being raised by their caretakers.

There is not one outcome superior to another. We don't land in our families by accident. The love, along with the angst, builds our life path. The richness from our familial experiences can be honored and recognized as being the foundation for our identity today. Family members are supreme teachers for us, guides. The bond is sacred because few other relationships have the depth of influence in our lives that our parents, sisters and brothers can provide for us. Well into adulthood they continue to teach us about our old triggers, our strengths, our capacity to love and heal, even in their absence.

Perhaps one of the greatest insights a family brings to us is the understanding that we have our own unique identities. We can inherit the family business or we can walk away serenaded by the protests of generations, but it is our choice. Self-fulfilling prophecies, like when a person consistently hears, "You're no good and you'll never amount to anything," may create severe confidence issues. We could choose to believe that we indeed can't accomplish a thing; however, this only works if we *choose to believe* in these prophecies, if we agree to them. They are powerful, no doubt, but many people have rejected the poisons of self-fulfilling prophecies, choosing not to accept that the expectations of others are an impenetrable fortress holding us captive. In fact, there are just as many cases of parents who raise their child with an onslaught of constant praise and accolade but the child grows up choosing to reject anything that looks even remotely like accomplishment. No one can control or predict that outcome; it's our choice.

We do inherit ancestral wounds and generational gifts, but we need not accept either unless we've chosen to do so. We're not implying it's an easy process to transform our inherited patterns—for some it is and for some it truly isn't—but we can choose something new. Regardless of whether our biological parents raised us or we were adopted or fostered, we've all inherited a life that has formed us today.

My (Kristy's) mother was detached, overwhelmed, chronically depressed, overweight and spent her entire short life believing she was helpless to change her situation. She died at the age of forty-eight. She was also an incredibly gifted artist and singer. She was egalitarian, creative, universally accepting and resourceful. My father was a severe alcoholic, a chain-smoker, chronic liar, close-minded, inappropriate and abusive on so many levels. He was also hilarious, loving, physically strong, an incredible athlete and dancer and just plain silly.

ARE WE ALLOWED TO CHOOSE WHAT WE ACCEPT FROM OUR HERITAGE?

In the enormous basket that holds all of these familial traits, I choose to believe that I have benefited by every one of them. There is no good or bad. They are all experiences, which have made me the incredibly strong, resourceful, creative, funny, caring, truth-loving, accepting and open-minded person I am today. That doesn't mean that I haven't undergone a tremendous evolution over the past forty years to find balance with all of them. But choosing to keep myself chained in one place by lamenting or obsessing over the one or many characteristics that didn't do right by me when I was twelve, isn't a plan of action that I ultimately chose. If I believe in my ultimate wholeness, my human divinity, I can choose to look at my life growing up as a series of powerful experiences, ones which molded my life to a sacred degree. My mother, my father, my siblings…they are all serving a purpose, divine beings expressing a number of roles, to support my evolution as a soul, just as I am to them. I was a hell-raiser as a teen. I partied a lot, I was anorexic, I was intensely defiant and I spent the majority of my time feeling intense anger toward my parents. Add those experiences to their soul-basket and I can look upon my teen experiences as simply a contribution to their evolution. Throughout my twenties I hated myself for how I had treated my parents. My mom died when I was only 19. I didn't have time to make amends for those unruly teen years. "Everyone goes through them," I was told. But it didn't matter. It felt right to punish myself at the time.

When I was originally informed that my mother had adenocarcinoma of the lungs, one of the most aggressive forms of metastatic malignant cancer, we were told that she had about six months to live. I worked at a B. Dalton Booksellers when I was eighteen, the time of her diagnosis, and I went about collecting all of the book titles I knew she'd need to beat this thing. *Anatomy of an Illness* by Norman Cousins, *Minding the Body, Mending the Mind* by Joan Borysenko, *Love, Medicine and Miracles* by Bernie Siegel and *You Can Heal Your Life* by Louise Hay. I was so certain that she only needed to read these books to turn away this army of devouring cancer cells. She read them. She enjoyed them. But she didn't stop the cancer. Infuriating! She wasn't trying, I was certain of it! She was choosing to leave me! To a young woman it was all so unfair. I only got angrier. And that too was a precious experience for me. I know now that regret is not something a divine being gets mired within. What if at that time I believed I could do no wrong? (Wait a minute. Most teens do feel that, don't they? I know I did. But what if rather than playing the role of the know-it-all, I had actually believed it with all of my wholeness?)

What would I have done at such a tender age, a teenager who had just lost her mother, but who possessed a conscious understanding of the S.T.A.R. philosophy? What would the experience have looked like had I accepted my own *Wholeness (human divinity)* and had accepted my mother's too? My navigation of those following years would have looked very differently. For example:

> *Surrender*—I would have surrendered to the truth that my mother as a divine being had chosen her time to die. I would have relinquished control and would have understood that her choice to not heal herself, which is what I had judged to have taken place, was entirely her right as a sovereign being. I would honor that her departure was a part of my destiny; a driving force for my future experiences. And honestly, even if

she had consciously chosen to abandon me, I would have respected this decision as hers to make.

Trust—I would have trusted that all was perfect, including the fact that I had been a typical teenager pushing the limits of my parental controlled boundaries prior to her diagnosis. My defiance, my under-aged drinking, my anorexia were all perfect manifestations of the life I had been born into. As above, so below. My chaos was a mirror reflection of the family chaos, expressed uniquely through my own experience.

Allow—I would have allowed my love for my mother to be primary, rather than focusing on the loss of her. Beyond that I would have been there for her through her experience, understanding that whatever she chose—to live or die—was an expression of her divinity.

Receive—I would have received the opening to evolve from this experience without struggling with feelings of regret, resentment, shame and abandonment, understanding that as an empowered divine being, my choices were the best I had at the time and my mother's experience belonged to her. It wasn't for me to fix or cure or make sense of. I would have received a great amount of peace from this.

The path I took at the time was the path of a frightened and heartbroken child who didn't have the conscious understanding of the tools for the new world. *And all was perfect as it was.* Each experience I collected through those painful years sculpted me into the graceful and fiery woman that I became. Looking back on that young nineteen year old who felt so alone, all I can do is shower her experience with understanding, total acceptance, unconditional love and the illumination of S.T.A.R. as it pertains to me today. Wholeness is not linear. We can go back in time to use this magic wand in any way we choose. I have chosen a new process, to embrace that scared young woman with the light of love rather than beat her with regret, shame and unforgiving. Punishment is not the work of the divine.

Is it humanly possible to become the Fascinated Observer through the process of witnessing a loved-one's death? Can it be done? We certainly can't ask or force another to live. We can offer our insights and share the tools that have assisted us through our darkest times, but ultimately the choice is personal. Can we ask a child to adopt a new worldview when they're crippled with grief? Becoming the Fascinated Observer through our life's most painful events is perhaps one of the most challenging tools to adopt and also the most healing. It's not about dissociating from the pain. That's not it at all. It's about fully feeling the pain, not fighting it. It's about witnessing our self as well as another and being with the circumstances without judgment, controlling, speculation or storytelling in order to avoid the emotions, be the "cure giver" or be the hero. It's about living in the moment rather than attaching to the future by attempting to force our desired outcome on the sovereign being who has selected that moment to exit this plane of existence.

Activity: Re-writing an Old Story

Take this moment to think of a powerful family memory, something that sticks with you today—painful or joyful—what comes to mind? Take some time and create a new story surrounding these circumstances in the form of a fairy tale with you as the protagonist. In stories, the angst is the driving force to liberation or renewal. Observe the angst in your story and commune with it. Create a new ending if you like, a new energy you'd like to carry, from the seed of the past. Do this with the intention of healing, honoring the memory as a crucial experience from which you have grown. Do this to "close the book."

Contemplate the possibility of sharing your fairy tale with an intimate friend or family member, but only if you feel you would like to. This is a deeply personal exercise and it's perfectly okay if you'd prefer to hold it close to your heart. The act of sharing such a vulnerable piece of you in the company of someone who honors you can also be transformative and validating.

Moving into Community and Expanding into the World

Some say that technology and media are isolating us rather than uniting us. That there is no substitute for sitting next to a person and hearing them breathe, smelling the coffee they're drinking and feeling them tap their foot to the song on the radio. This may be true to some degree. Personally, when Nina and I are having a videoconference conversation with other like-minded individuals across the globe, it becomes such a somatic experience for us that they may as well be seated right beside us. What it takes to connect can mean something different to each person. And the level to which we connect is also highly variable. There are those who surround themselves with so many friends they can barely keep track of everybody. Others go through their entire lives with only one or two deep connections. There is no right or wrong when defining our communities. For some, communities are nearly a hundred percent online. For others, it's in person or nothing. One thing is certain though and that is that human beings require some sense of community for optimum wellness.

Sociologists Debra Umberson and Jennifer Karas Montez recently published a study titled "Social Relationships and Health: A Flashpoint for Health Policy." (Umberson and Montez, 2011) through the National Institutes of Health. Their research found that *positive social relationships strongly affect our health and our mortality.* Those with low social ties or poor-quality relationships were tied to a higher correlation of medical conditions including development and progression of cardiovascular disease, heart attack, stroke, hardening of the arteries, autoimmune disorders, high blood pressure, cancer and delayed cancer recovery and slower wound healing. Famed medical researcher Dr. Dean Ornish in his book, *Love and Survival*, writes that lack of social support is a health risk factor as risky as smoking, living a sedentary existence and eating a diet high in saturated fat.

When we connect to the current of self-love which is critical to establishing a connection with ourselves, we find that our external relationships become stronger and more nurturing. We obtain richness through human connection which translates biologically, psychologically, emotionally and spiritually. Let your support system be what you need. When we feel that support beneath us, we're empowered and strengthened.

THE TELEPATHIC SUPER-HIGHWAY

Have you ever thought about somebody you haven't seen in decades, a random memory popping into your consciousness with no prompting and then within a short period of time this person actually contacts you? A dear friend of ours has dubbed synchronicities like this "freaky cool," a term I (Kristy) have permanently adopted. At quantum particle level this type of phenomenon is called *nonlocality*, and it means that an invisible field of energy, a super-highway, through which we can reach out and communicate with anyone at any time, connects us all. Nonlocality could end up explaining the freaky cool stuff of synchronicity, when unexplained coincidences happen that are just too incredible to explain away to chance.

I once had the desire to learn more about Tarot. I went to Barnes and Noble in Minneapolis and bought a book/DVD set that I hoped could teach me a little about this ancient intuitive art. It was called *The Tarot Discovery Kit* by Amy Zerner and Monte Farber, famous intuitives about whom I knew nothing. I took it home and settled into my cozy couch in my family room, multi-tasking by streaming my Facebook wall while I perused the details of my new Tarot set. As I read the instructions, I noticed that somebody had friended me on my Facebook page. Distracted, I clicked onto the notification to find that the friend request came from Amy Zerner herself, the author of this kit I had just bought! What the…I couldn't even fathom it. I immediately sent her a message, "How…why…by what reason did you friend me in this very moment, when I had no idea who you even were prior to sitting down to explore this newly purchased Tarot stuff? How do you even know who I am?" I asked, wanting a solid left-brain analytical answer to explain this mind-blowing experience, but she wrote back only one sentence, "Don't you just love synchronicities?" And that was it—freaky cool indeed!

Develop your own telepathic super-highway. Over the next few days think about a good friend you haven't spoken with in awhile. Set the intention that they reach out to you in some way within a set period of time. Every day schedule a few minutes to really connect with this person through thought. Note what takes place. If they haven't contacted you within your set time frame, consider making the connection yourself.

When I (Kristy) moved to Santa Fe a few years ago I thought I had died and gone to heaven. Perhaps I had. I remember first rolling into town and shortly thereafter stocking my new kitchen with groceries. I was in Whole Foods that day, feeling my way to a perfect avocado, when I suddenly looked up at all the people in the produce section. Something welled up within me! "These are my people!" I silently gushed, getting all sappy right where I stood. None of them knew me and that didn't matter. I felt their energy and I wanted to be a part of this! It was my first experience with the sensation of "fitting in." Having lived in Colorado, Texas, Minnesota and New Hampshire, I had enjoyed aspects of all of them, even dearly loved some of them, but this connection was brand new to me. It was as if we were all inhaling and exhaling in perfect harmony. I have loved the states I've lived in before, but my relationship with New Mexico was the first experience I had with the reciprocity of feeling a state *actually loving me back!* It was a magical moment for me, this realization.

Feeling that sense of unity is how I define community. Others find that unity through a church or a baseball team or a band, a hiking group or an astronomy club. Pick your connection; it's there. We truly believe that this type of connection between people can be made side by side or thousands of miles away, with technology the link to our communication. What would it take for you to deepen your sense of community? Perhaps you feel as though it's perfect as it is?

Can I Truly, Openly Share?

Somebody shared a sentiment with us recently. She said, "*I have never told anyone that I saw angels when I was young. I didn't know with whom I could possibly share this.*"

So many times in my (Nina's) travels around the planet, I have heard similar remarks. We have not felt safe to share our inner wisdom, our transcendent experiences or our other than how-it-is-supposed-to-be stories. Perhaps it is because our cellular memory remembers the times that we were burned at the stake for speaking our truth. Perhaps it is because we were discredited, scolded or told that we were wrong when we spoke of our visions. No longer! We have entered a new paradigm and it is time to speak and share our inner wisdom and to feel safe in another's presence as we do so.

Thousands of people across the planet have done just that. A safe space, the Gathering of Golden Dolphins, was created June 5, 2011 in Santa Fe, New Mexico, for star seeds to gather to talk about the Four Essential Qualities. There was never judgment, only deep listening and graceful speaking. Those golden dolphins who gathered felt at ease in the presence of other divine humans who validated and loved them even though they might have been strangers. Over the year that we met, we got stronger and stronger in our sharing with each other. I refer to this growth as "strengthening our human divinity muscle."

Growing new muscles was important to do in community, where we felt supported and most importantly safe. Then with strong new muscles, we found that we were able to go outside of our circles into the world and stand tall, no longer *knowing* ourselves as divine, but *accepting* ourselves as sovereign beings. We found that safety was coming from within and that we no longer needed to seek it from our external reality. We were in a space of deep inner peace.

So many times in my (Nina's) travels around the planet, I have heard The Gatherings of Golden Dolphins, which formed in South Africa, in Egypt, in Israel, in the United Kingdom, in the Netherlands…were a catalyst for moving the evolution of humanity from knowing to accepting. We came together in safe spaces, in community and we honored the divine in all present. What I discovered from this experience is that when I am with another person, I will hold the intention that they feel safe in my presence. This is critically important because the time is now for us to dream together our vision of the new earth. Our words and thoughts freely shared are tools for co-creating that dream.

Do we allow those around us to be their own authentic self? Or do we find reasons to separate one community from another, bringing in old paradigms of right and wrong, better and worse, higher and lower? There's a whole lot of head-butting going on today between individuals, communities, states, countries... If we think about S.T.A.R. as being a tool for living in the new earth, what is asking to be transformed?

EVERYTHING IS A METAPHOR

More than once throughout our history (at the time of writing this paragraph), the United States government has completely shut down. Two parties unable to communicate, unable to see the other's point of view, unable to provide any kind of safe space for connection due to the politics of one community against another, one party having to come out ahead; win! Their actions, the origin of which can be reduced down to just a few men and women exerting their control against those less resolved and more malleable, were having a widespread effect on hundreds of communities across the United States and indeed across the world. It's true as we accept S.T.A.R. that, *all is perfect* and we can observe with fascination what these events trigger in all of us. But how can we activate our own divinity to create something new from the wreckage of similar breakdowns if we choose?

It is not naive to visualize the governing bodies of the Unites States transitioning from the old world paradigm into something brand new, elected men and women who know what it means to create a safe environment for all ideas, all peoples, all communities, all concepts to be discussed. Indeed it seems that at this juncture they are demonstrating the absolute stagnant nature of old paradigm ways asking for a metamorphosis. At times it feels they are fighting for the sake of the fight. The issues are irrelevant. "I'm against what he's for, no matter what that is!" Right? What if we flexed our human divinity muscles and dreamed something different?

As a beautiful example, let's envision something as powerful as the United States government, exerting its influence across the globe, affecting too many communities to count, undergoing a S.T.A.R. transformation. What would that look like to you?

To us it might look something like this. First of all, every member of the U.S. Congress would be fully aligned with the Four Essential Qualities. (Oh, we *can* dream this into reality! Until then, it's just plain fun. Let's go wild with this.) Each elected person would accept their *Wholeness (human divinity)*. They would live their sovereignty unable or unwilling to take influence from another no matter how many dollar signs were attached to it. They would have a strong foundation in *Self-love*, so much so that they would never think about that next election or what they have to compromise within themselves in order to gain a vote. (Think about it!) If they lost popularity based on their authentic beliefs, so be it. They'd accept that too.

CAN FANTASIZING START THE PROCESS OF CREATIVE MOMENTUM?

*Continue on with our fantasy...*Next, each member of the U.S. government would be fully connected to *Play (the now moment)*. Fulfilling their civic duty would bring them joy and they would consider it play. They would never have concern about the politics of elections because they'd be living each moment present and accountable to what is happening in the world right now! And lastly and this is a big one, they would live and breathe the *Embodiment of the Expanded Golden Rule*. For the sake of a dollar, industries would not be allowed to poison our air, our drinking water, the foods we eat, and new technologies would be allowed to bloom which would not negatively impact the world's precious wildlife, our natural resources, our virgin forests. Communication would improve exponentially when we all learn to listen, to respect alternative viewpoints and allow another to have their say with rapt attention.

Of course the world is complicated! Of course its problems are complex! But what if simply visualizing this new way of being changed one person's point of view, one influential person, who somehow found a way to exert their positive influence on the person next to them? And like dominoes, we would watch as the whole world morphed into something beyond what we imagined. The United States, the United Kingdom, Saudi Arabia, India, Iran, China, North Korea, France… and on and on.

When the Four Essential Qualities ignite, then we can watch the radiance of S.T.A.R. catch fire across the planet. Suddenly there are no more government shut-downs. Politics fizzle out and what's left are 535 men and women, 536 with the President (100 in the Senate, 435 in the House), who are able to *Surrender* to the understanding that they are at an impasse. A new way of thinking will be required, they'll understand. They'll have to *Trust* what their fellow congress people have to say, knowing that each of them is coming from a place of authenticity and divinity, no ulterior motives to reveal or deny. They will *Allow* for alternative views, new ideas, novel concepts based on an atmosphere of safety and non-judgment; the place where innovation occurs every day across the world. And when they come to an acceptable outcome, knowing that crossing their arms, pursing their lips and putting their head in the sand is no longer an option, they will *Receive* new answers, new policies and the people of the world will receive the supreme example from the stars of their country.

Activity: Wave Your Magic Wand

Pick an existing institution and create something entirely new! Just as we've transformed the U.S. government here, you do the same with any organization that comes to mind for you. Some possibilities would be the educational system, the health care system, the pharmaceutical industry, the World Health

Organization, the United Nations or something much closer to home such as your workplace, your family unit or even your neighborhood bowling league!

Create a new vision for how your organization will operate under the S.T.A.R. philosophy, bringing into it the Four Essential Qualities of *Wholeness (human divinity)*, *Self-love*, *Play (the now moment)* and the *Embodiment of the Expanded Golden Rule*.

Journal your vision with an open heart, and listen with great awareness to your own dreams and desires to create something new. When you are finished, meditate on your own, truly anchoring in your body what it would feel like for your vision to become the new reality.

The relationships we cultivate with our own self and the people in our lives are best built on a foundation of empowerment. We empower others by respectfully giving them the space to create and choose, just as we can take total ownership of our own experiences. We don't have to like every experience or pretend what occurs is not excruciatingly painful at times, but regardless, we can choose to find in those experiences the useful inspiration they imparted to us. How do our experiences make us stronger, wiser or more loving? Let's play with these concepts by envisioning complete sovereignty in our life and the world around us.

CHAPTER FIVE:
ALL MY RELATIONS

AND WHAT OF OUR CONNECTION WITH THE NON-HUMAN world? Who are we without the animal community, without the trees or the flower kingdom? What wisdom lies within the great family of rocks, crystals and stones that have been called the historians of our planet, the keepers of the secrets of humanity? Where would we be without the bodies of water, our rivers, streams, lakes, ponds and oceans? Perhaps most of us understand their *uses to us*, but beyond that how many understand their critical importance as members of our community? The not-so-obvious gifts they bring to us which lie under their surface are perhaps their greatest gifts of all, the ones we tend to overlook. We used to know their place in our balance. Many still do. In our past, across the world, we have periodically gone to sleep, collectively. We have made choices. We have allowed industry to discharge unquantified levels of toxins into our sky and to pour deadly poisons straight into our waters. What experiences we have chosen…Skies blackened and rivers caught fire and then we pulled together to make different choices. It's just what we do.

A trend is happening in which many of us are marveling that everything in creation is alive, is sentient. Humanity can become whole again through this understanding. In Carol Schaefer's book, *Grandmothers Counsel the World*, she writes of the famed Thirteen Indigenous Grandmothers and their prophesies for our time and beyond. She says, "Though the prophecies that speak of great changes to earth are dire, the Grandmothers believe that the times will only affect those who do not heed the warnings. They say people will need physical, mental, emotional and spiritual strength to change themselves; otherwise a huge portion of the population will suffer immeasurably. Sadly, because the majority of humanity is not spiritually but instead materially oriented, it is feared that many people's reaction to the immense stress of the times, which they might not be able to handle emotionally, will be to destroy everything around them."

Understanding that we as divine humans are creator beings, capable of building a new reality, let us work to pour our love into the earth. Let us choose to respect the natural world as a sentient being. Using the *Embodiment of the Expanded Golden Rule*, let's build our relationship with nature and listen to the conversation taking place every day within the sentient world around us. Ecuador has recently written a new constitution which recognizes the legal rights of Mother Earth. Imagine! Suddenly Mother Earth finds herself in need of a consultant to understand the legal jargon, but how incredibly powerful this message is to the rest of the world. Fascinating.

ALL MY RELATIONS: THE ANIMAL KINGDOM

Depending upon from what part of the world you originate, animals may or may not play a crucial role in your community. To some cultures they are completely overlooked and ignored, their domesticity considered totally bizarre at best, disgusting at worst. In other countries, they are a multi-billion dollar industry. Between veterinary medicine, pet supplies in the form of food, clothing, toys, beds and supplements, as well as boarding facilities, training facilities, breeders…we Americans shell out billions of dollars a year to keep our domesticated animals cozy, healthy and comfortable. We dress them up for Halloween, make them cakes for their birthdays, feature them on our holiday cards and pay artists to immortalize them through any number of media. We are absolutely bonkers for our four-legged babies.

Our need to infantilize them notwithstanding, their greatest gifts often go unnoticed by their families. Far wiser than many give them credit for, in many cases they're treated as just an obligation or a piece of living art, something which brings us comfort, such that we often fail to pay much attention to creating a stimulating life for them. Animal communication—actually conversing with animals—is often depicted in our media as ludicrous, a ridiculous joke. Perhaps this is a symptom of our collective disconnection? Why is it so silly for some to recognize the innate ability of our animals to communicate with us? Perhaps if it weren't so, we'd have to consider our collective treatment of them throughout our history. Maybe it makes us feel better to consider them "dumb animals."

Our anthropocentric tendency to consider humans the only species to have the capacity for thought has been unraveling for decades. Scientific studies have become plentiful in the area of animal intelligence. The higher primates (apes and Old World monkeys such as baboons), cetaceans (whales and dolphins), African grey parrots and cockatoos, the corvidae species of birds (crows, ravens, magpies, etc.) and even common pigs have been found to have incredible problem-solving capacities, tool-usage skills and staggeringly high intelligence far beyond what we typically attribute to these creatures. Perhaps, if we opened to the full acceptance of their magnificence as sentient, intelligent, spiritual beings, we would have to take a painful inventory of how we've treated them across the planet. Can we fully open to the concept of the *Embodiment of the Expanded Golden Rule* to include the animal kingdom? What will shift across the planet when we collectively embody the philosophy of "do unto all creatures what I would have done unto me"? What will shift within your own life?

I (Kristy) have a favorite story I love to tell, which happened a couple of years ago. I lived in a small mountain town in New Mexico at the time and a brutal winter blizzard was pounding us. I was huddled up on the couch, early in the morning, tightly tucked in with a big cozy blanket and was still freezing. My Saluki dog, Arya, was curled up on a recliner chair across the room. She seemed comfortable enough. I was quietly complaining in my head, no other human home to hear me. The space heater was four feet away from me, sitting unused. I really wanted to turn it on, but I didn't want to get out from my cozy blanket cocoon! I stared at it just sitting there, taunting my laziness. "I wish that thing would *turn on*!" I whined telepathically. Just then, Arya uncurled and stood up on her chair. She arched her back into a big stretch and hopped off. Sauntering across the room, still half-asleep, she headed straight for the space heater. Without hesitating, she bumped the big "on" switch with her nose. It fired right up and began oscillating its glorious heat! Without pausing, she turned around and sauntered back to her chair, all the while my mouth hanging open and my eyes bugging out of my head. Requiring no accolades, she curled back up and closed her eyes. No big deal to her; she just wanted my whining to stop. I was completely blown away! Shocked! I began howling with incredulous laughter, wishing somebody had been there to experience this phenomenon with me! No matter how I could try to deconstruct what happened as "chance" or coincidence (something my left-analytical brain loves to do), I couldn't do it. It was just too incredible!

The extraordinary telepathic capacity of animals should have come as no surprise to me. They live their life as the world's "receivers," teaching us how to expand our intuition and telepathy if we'll only pay attention to how it's done. They have to utilize their extra-sensory perception if they expect to stay alive in the wild. They're expert psychics, each and every one, and it's as unremarkable as breathing for them.

In 2004 the world experienced the deadliest tsunami in history, which took place in Indonesia. Across the world over 200,000 people died as a result of this catastrophic event. One of the most curious aspects of this oceanic earthquake was the fact that very few animals were found dead in the aftermath. In post-disaster interviews, witnesses recalled that prior to the tsunami striking, numbers of wild animals such as elephants and monkeys were seen high-tailing it to higher ground. They clearly sensed the looming danger and thus the subsequent death toll for them was low. Now who is superior to whom?

We can choose to believe that animals wild and domestic are sovereign beings. Animals and humans alike carry incredible gifts. We can observe that humans are far more advanced in many areas of existence and animals are far more advanced in others. But the entire conversation about superiority is irrelevant. We as humans have chosen to develop certain capacities and they as animals, have chosen to develop others. As a team, we have all the bases covered! Who's keeping score?

Gandhi said, "The greatness of a nation and its moral progress can be judged by the way in which its animals are treated." Let's expand that to the entire planet. It's important to understand that if we are going to live by the Four Essential Qualities, one of which is adopting the *Embodiment of the Expanded Golden Rule*—do unto all creatures as we would have done unto us—then we must take an internal inventory of where we can raise our octaves in relation to our treatment of our animal sisters and brothers, wild and domesticated. It's also important to align with our *Wholeness (human divinity)* in understanding that *all is perfect*. It's an old-paradigm third-dimensional practice to rally against something. Rather, as we increase our evolutionary octave and step into the new-paradigm living, we can focus on making different choices. We dream something new into existence and work to make it so. Collectively, we created all that is in this moment in time throughout our history and into our future. So, when we discover

IS IT POSSIBLE TO ABSOLUTELY MEASURE SENTIENCE?

what falls outside of the Four Essential Qualities, we invoke our *Wholeness (human divinity)* and make the choice to make something new! Something that feels more heart-centered and sustainable to every sentient being on our beautiful planet.

ALL MY RELATIONS: THE ENVIRONMENT

Through his water research, Dr. Masaru Emoto writes about *hado*, the energy or vibration inherent in all things. He taught us that through our interaction with water (we are after all mostly water ourselves) we can learn to send the energy of love to all beings across the planet. Burying our feet in the dirt grounds us and the frequencies of certain crystals send us soaring. There are those who can't be in the presence of crystals without feeling dizzy and light-headed. Scrambling over boulders within the Rocky Mountains makes us feel strong as granite in the high altitude, which makes us feel dense and heavy. Resting in the shade of an apple tree cools us and the sun warms us. Flowers and roots are medicinal, caring for us long before we dreamed our current pharmaceutical industry into existence. Our connection to our environment is very much communal. Without it, we feel disconnected, depressed, robotic, and many go as far as to say they feel "dead" when forced to live within a concrete jungle.

Indigenous, shamanic or totemic cultures have long lived by their relationship with the environment. Caring for the *tree-people* and the *rock-people* and the *plant-people,* while acknowledging the water spirits or the air spirits, has been the way of life for cultures all over our planet since the dawn of time. Thunderbeings aren't just the sounds that lightning makes; they're powerful beings who watch over us and care for us. And fire is the ultimate purifier, the cleanser of old energies.

To some degree all of us have indigenous origins, no matter if our people originated in Asia or Europe or the Americas, we all bloomed from native roots. The knowledge of the interconnection of all the sentient beings that comprise our environment is a remembering that we can all feel, some more strongly than others. I (Kristy) myself had a stick as a friend when I was a child. I carried it everywhere, talked to it, felt comforted by it. When my brother took my stick and hurled it javelin-style into Lake Superior, I watched as it drifted farther and farther away from me and sobbed like he had just thrown away my own life-force. Utterly confused, he mumbled, "Jeeze. Why don't you just have a stick as your brother then." I screamed, "I can't! You just threw it in the lake!" Touché. Kids feel the interconnection, the *hado*, all around us and are supremely sensitive to that life force. So much so, that there is a theory today called Nature Deficit Disorder caused by the reliance on technology to entertain our children rather than giving them the freedom to roam around outside, losing themselves in the marvels of nature. According to author/journalist Richard Louv, Nature Deficit Disorder is caused by the many temptations of the video screen, fearful parents who are not comfortable allowing their kids to run around outside unsupervised and loss of natural habitats which results in anxiety, depression and decreased ability to focus and concentrate. It's a fascinating hypothesis, the implications of which are worth considering.

What have we lost if we've disconnected with our environment as a legitimate member of our community? If we can't see the life force in all of creation, then it's much easier to disregard it. How would it change us to learn to speak *to* the environment around us rather than *about* it? If we learned to have conversations with trees, would we be so inclined to chop them down for cultural convenience? The South American rain forests and the great coral reefs have been termed the "lungs of the world" with their incredible role of filtering our atmosphere. If we learned to hear the wisdom from the coral reefs, would we treat them with more respect? S.T.A.R. asks us to respectfully take our place in the community of Mother Earth.

UNIVERSAL COSMIC CONNECTIONS

Can we allow others their unique experiences? What of the countless millions who have reported their experiences with angels, faeries or extra-terrestrials? I know somebody who claims to have found her way into a grove of woodland faeries as a young adult! She conversed with them! This person is completely grounded today and is a top executive at a Fortune 500 company. She insists that this memory had nothing to do with imagination. It happened in the physical realm and no mind-altering substances were involved! Can we allow our minds to utter the words "What if?" How do we navigate these experiences, especially when we're listening to the story of another, without judgment clouding our senses?

Is there a reason why millions of people spend their hard-earned dollars on psychics, channeled books, DVDs, podcasts, as well as classes and online courses surrounding the metaphysics of spirit communication? We're not *all* crazy, are we? Why do we love movies like E.T. and Peter Pan? Ask anyone—give them the safe space to answer authentically, free of judgment—and they'll share a story of totally unexplained phenomena with you. They will share something which maybe happened fifty years ago or just last week, which has completely shifted their experience of being human. For me (Kristy) the first experience happened when I was eighteen months old. Three spirits visited me when I was still in my crib. In the middle of the night, they peered over me as I lay silent and helpless, listening to them discuss me. My parents just ten feet away, sound asleep, heard or experienced nothing. And though I was still in diapers, sleeping in a bassinet, I remember it with crystal clarity. The world cracked open for me that night and things unseen entered my reality. I have never met anyone during my existence who doesn't have a similar experience. The details may vary greatly, but the mechanism is the same, which is that something enormous took place, something beyond the confines of the everyday experience and the fear of rejection or ridicule caused us to protect this experience, keep it a secret, rather than share it.

Activity: Your Super Powers

Making universal cosmic connections is accomplished by opening to our innate gifts. Take a moment to ponder your super powers. You know you have them! What makes you different from everyone else; what are your secret gifts? Create a superhero persona for yourself and claim it as you! Have fun with this. Journal all of the details of this new facet of you, be extravagant with your vision. When finished, create a small artistic representation of your superhero identity, be it a painting, a drawing, a collage, an edited digital image or anything else you can imagine and put it in a place where it can be viewed daily as a constant reminder of your super powers.

Don't be afraid
to accept
your own
magnificence

BEYOND TYPICAL CHARACTERIZATIONS

Living the role of the Fascinated Observer allows us to accept the truth that human beings have never known every secret to the cosmos, so what creates the human tendency to mark another person's experience as false, untrue, ludicrous or insane? If I'm not afraid of you with all of your differences from me, why would I be afraid of things unexplained? Why would I have any need to characterize them as normal or abnormal? Does it even matter any longer?

And what of the ethics of our Universal cosmic connections, as they relate to actual space? What is our place in the Universe? According to which study you read, it has been documented that up to two-thirds of Americans believe that some form of alien life exists across the span of our Universe. In a recent United Kingdom survey, more people believe in extra-terrestrials than in God. Our solar system alone is so vast that according to an article published in *Universe Today* even NASA's *New Horizons*, the fastest spacecraft ever launched from earth, would require 37,000 years of travel before it reached the edge. The Milky Way galaxy contains around 200 billion stars, and is one of at least 100 billion galaxies in the known Universe. It's an enormous Universe, so what are the odds that we're flying solo here, that only our precious planet earth sustains any form of life? What do you believe and why is this a controversial subject for us? Isn't it a reasonable conversation to have? Nobody claims to have any definitive answer, yet for some a direct ticket to crazy town is earned by openly espousing a belief in life outside of planet earth. It really is fascinating!

Take a moment to contemplate a few questions on space ethics and if you choose, discuss your views with others. There are no right or wrong answers, these are simply designed to have fun with your critical thinking:

⊙ What do you think about launching our garbage into outer space, including some of the most toxic chemicals on the planet?

⊙ Do you agree with the plans to terraform Mars, which is the act of deliberately modifying the planet's ecosystem to support human life?

⊙ Do you believe in a cosmic version of manifest destiny, whereby human beings should be allowed to take any action on any existing planet in order to further our own wellbeing?

⊙ What should happen if another life form exists and finds its way to earth? How would you receive such an experience?

⊙ Should space travel be exploited for the extremely rich?

⊙ If a plan to inhabit another planet was put into place, would you volunteer to go?

⊙ If other life forms do exist, would you be more receptive to them if they appeared somewhat humanoid? If their appearance was horrifying to you, would this affect your reception of them?

Activity: Examining Storylines

Think about the countless dollars that Hollywood has earned from our fascination with life beyond earth. Choose one of the following films or pick your own to contemplate the Essential Qualities as they relate to the storyline.

- *2001: A Space Odyssey*
- *Alien*
- *Avatar*
- *Close Encounters of the Third Kind*
- *Cocoon*
- *District 9*
- *Enemy Mine*
- *E.T.*
- *Forbidden Planet*
- *Independence Day*
- *K-PAX*
- *Men in Black*
- *Stargate*
- *Starman*
- *Signs*
- *War of the Worlds*

You can use this activity for a group movie night! Gather, watch and then discuss your revelations with others.

After watching, consider:

- How do you see *Wholeness (human divinity)*, *Self-love*, *Play (the now moment)* and the *Embodiment of the Expanded Golden Rule* playing a part in the storyline?

- How would you have navigated this experience if you were asked to live it, using the S.T.A.R. philosophy and the Four Essential Qualities?

SAFETY AND VULNERABILITY

As Eckhart Tolle says in his book *A New Earth*, as the new consciousness emerges and is birthed into our world, many people will feel the need to form groups to mirror this new consciousness. Within our own informal S.T.A.R. discussion groups, we have witnessed something extraordinary. These groups are made of individuals, sovereign beings, who began by looking to Nina to lead them. As the groups evolved, they began to not look to one person to lead them, but a melding of minds formed to share solutions to even the most ancient problems. Rather than from a primitive collective form, which is what we find in "mob mentalities" in which humans can be capable of committing atrocities that they would never consider as an individual, these new-paradigm groups comprise those who don't seek their identity through the collective. The shame or embarrassment about sharing their thoughts magically disappears. Bonds of respect are formed. We can stand in our own power, with the knowing that nobody can do anything *to us*, for we are sovereign beings creating what we wish to experience. Our first communities formed through wholeness and heart, forming a new way of being together in shaping our world.

Synergy refers to a combined action of elements resulting in a total effect that is greater than all those elements standing independently. Our wish is that in the future we create synergy in all of our newly formed communities across this great planet of ours, offering our unique experiences and views in an extraordinary way. Vietnamese Zen Buddhist monk, author and teacher Thich Nhat Hanh has been quoted saying, "It is possible that the next Buddha will not take the form of an individual. The next Buddha may take the form of a community, a community practicing understanding and loving kindness, a community practicing mindful living. And the practice can be carried out as a group, as a city, as a nation." We're coming together in sovereignty.

IS SURRENDER AN ACT OF COURAGE OR VULNERABILITY?

An essential ingredient in creating this new world of heart-centered communities is the freedom to be transparent. Moving beyond the status quo of judgment, argument and wars will require transparency to solidify a new foundation of being. Perhaps we can begin this process by asking, "To what do I give power?" Is it our need to be *right*? Is it our need that we believe we must battle that which is *wrong*? Where has that pattern taken us, collectively?

In *S. T.A. R. Philosophy*, Nina identifies the three components of growth as being permission, validation and safety. Imagine a conversation in which you are granted all three. It's fairly easy to open up to our own authenticity in such a container, isn't it? Being given the permission to be exactly who we are and to say exactly what we believe, having the validation to speak our thoughts with no judgment or ridicule, provides the absolute safety, which is critical as the octaves we experience expand and contract. Safety is what it's all about. With safety, we are allowed divine license to become who we wish to be. The greatest gifts we can give to each other are permission, validation and safety. With this foundation, we find the courage to become vulnerable.

Can growth occur without vulnerability? Can relationships bloom without it? To go through life unwilling to experience vulnerability means we march through our experiences with armor on. Compressed and protected, running in circles, we are forever looking out for the next great pain all the while devising a way to avoid it. In navigating away from the judgment of "painful" experiences, we make the decision to avoid vulnerability altogether. The expression of that looks like a life protected and walled, we carry a shell around with us, encasing our heart, which others can see and feel. Have you ever met a person with so many internal walls that you immediately turn the other way? Your first impression is, "Wow. I don't have the power to permeate armor as dense as that, so what's the point in trying?" The path of least resistance dictates that we simply move on to someone else, not so armored. The quest to avoid vulnerability generally results in a lonely or boring life. It's the old cliché about finding the full vitality of life by stepping outside our comfort zone, which is where vulnerability tends to hang out.

My co-author, Nina Brown, has recently adopted a vulnerability exercise. Every day she does something outside her comfort zone, for the sake of growth and expansion. Her daily practice is nothing incredibly disruptive, but it's proven to be powerful. One day she purchased a bright pink leopard bra from Victoria's Secret! Another day she took a short mountain hike all alone. On another day she took a field trip to a state senator's office to gift him a book. Every time we stretch into a new place, the cost of the journey a few tender nerves or a little knot in our stomach, we grow. We find greater strength from which to build a new caliber of relationships all around us.

Activity: Miracle Memories

Is there an experience from your past that you have been afraid to share? Something your analytical brain can't explain, something you keep secret for fear of being seen as wacky or crazy? Perhaps this experience (or these experiences) changed your life in some way?

If you have many memories of this nature, pick one that seems to be the *loudest* in this moment. Sit in silent contemplation with this memory. To whom or what do you credit this communication? Was this experience delivered to you from your angels, your transitioned loved ones or perhaps you attribute them to archetypal energies, archangels, God (whatever your language might be) or the pure expression of your own human divinity? Recall the magnificence of the miracle and give thanks for it as a profound gift.

In your home, create a small altar or place something on your existing altar, which honors this memory. If there is a certain entity you attribute your memory to, honor whomever it may be by including an image or object to signify him/her/it. Sit with your altar every day, perhaps lighting a candle or playing powerful music for a selected period of time, with the intention of honoring the miracles all around us and our will to see them and accept them as a pure extension of our own divinity. Watch what begins to shift in your life as you connect with this sacred ritual.

THE FULL SCOPE

Connections are essential to the human spirit while safety and vulnerability are foundational elements in building a circle of those connections. The full scope of our relationships emerges first in the form of self-love and then into our relationships with family, communities, worldviews and our interconnection to all sentient beings in the cosmos including our environment itself.

Here we have stretched ourselves by considering conversations with animals, trees and rocks and then took it further by expanding into the cosmos and beyond, discussing our possible relationships with angels, spirits and creatures from the faerie realms or other places in the cosmos. To experience the full scope of relationships from this perspective, we are tasked with establishing a secure and practical connection with our own divinity and experimenting with being a sovereign being. Self-love is an integral aspect guiding our journey to divinity. Here we practice the art of walking our path as the Fascinated Observer to sustain our ability to express self-love. We can *Surrender* to the concept of OUR divinity, that all creatures are sovereign beings having their own spiritual experience, *Trust* that we can live in synergy as we form new communities of supportive souls, *Allow* others to be their own glorious selves without judgment or condescension and *Receive* the beauty of the new world, a heart-centered, interconnected, global community of love consciousness.

Are you ready to create more of this in your life? We are so ready to create more of it in ours.

Part Three:
The Fascinated Octaves of Wellbeing

TRUE WELLBEING

From *S.T.A.R. Philosophy* by Nina Brown (pages 156–157)

The body communicates information to us in numerous ways. Illness and pain are two ways with which we are familiar. They cause us to move out of a subconscious way of being and to pay attention to our body or our environment. Our first reaction is to take or do something that will return us to "normal." Perhaps that normal no longer serves us and we should begin to allow new solutions to emerge.

S.T.A.R. wisdom allows us to no longer strive to control our environment and our body, but to observe in fascination what is causing the conditions or symptoms that we are experiencing. Is there something out of alignment in how our body is expressing its current experience? Is there a life lesson that is whispering or even shouting at us that we need to learn? Is our personality running the show and overloading our bodies with an ever-increasing supply of chemicals in response to negative thoughts?

The most powerful tool that we have in applying S.T.A.R. wisdom to our wellbeing, is metacognition. We can observe our condition and make a conscious choice to respond appropriately. We can be a conscious observer of our body, our environment and our thoughts and feelings about the reality in which we are having our current experience. What is serving us and what is not serving us?

When we begin to ask those questions, then we can react before our body or environment talks to us in shocking ways to get our attention. We are moving into a stage of conscious evolution; where in knowing our sovereignty we can author our future by choice and willful participation instead of through the subconscious, reactive mode fostered by an unbalanced ego. Is it possible that what we perceive as being in "un-wellness" is the perfect state of being at a precise moment in time on our journey?

Might the condition be sending us a message? How many times have we heard or read about situations where a life-threatening illness or event trans-formed the individual? They grew in consciousness in ways that astounded those around them. Was this a good thing or was it a bad thing? Or perhaps it just was a chosen experience. We might even want to suggest that the state of un-wellness was chosen as an exit door for the individual to pass beyond the physical state of consciousness expressing, to other realms of consciousness expressing. As we grow in awareness of who we truly are, perhaps we will be able to choose to transition without dis-ease, but by the mere ease of choice.

CHAPTER SIX:
REFINING THE MEANING OF MENTAL WELLBEING

IS MENTAL WELLBEING SOMETHING WE STRIVE TO ACHIEVE or acquire or is it simply a letting go of expectations and attachments to painful thought patterns? Is it a simple allowing of our own divinity to unfold and express? The S.T.A.R. philosophy is an incredible tool for defining and refining our meaning of wellbeing. When we can be the Fascinated Observer in our life, we implicitly trust that one experience is not superior to another. All of our experiences are presented to us as opportunities to grow and expand into the development of the greatest expression of our divinity. No matter what our path in life, we are all choosing our experiences based on what we are committed to understand in this life's expression. We can be so easily seduced by or get caught up in the "stories" of our mental processing; perhaps we identify as the broken one, the wounded one, the land-of-misfit toys version of ourselves, which actually can be valuable perspectives. But once we tap into the field of potentiality and affirm our right as a divine sovereign being to choose any reality for ourselves, the illusion of "brokenness" as a character default falls away. Any waters we happen to be navigating are integrally important, no matter how choppy, tumultuous or placid they might be. The Fascinated Observer knows this truth and can choose to detach from their own self-constructs of judgment. We are all precious, no matter what our illusions of brokenness have been. Take a moment and say this out loud, "I am precious." That's a step toward wellbeing, even if it takes some hard work to actually believe it or own it. Some find the words difficult to even speak.

Activity: The New-Thought Bracelet

Sometimes it's hard to comprehend that our recurring thought patterns are merely a chemical cocktail of neuropeptides to which our brain has become addicted. Everything is a drug to our mental wiring. A step toward rewiring our brains to become addicted to a new-thought chemical cocktail is to recognize when we're seeking a fix from the old thought. Try this for one week and see what it starts to shift. It's called using a *thought-stopping technique* and it's a powerful tool.

○ Wear a bracelet or a woven string on your wrist for seven days (or longer if you choose). This should be something you've chosen as a talisman to help you shift this energy; it can be elaborate, something with a crystal imbedded to assist you, or it can be supremely simple.

○ Whenever you hear yourself going into a destructive thought pattern, such as "I am not worthy. I look like an idiot!" stop the ruminations by gently handling the bracelet. Put your hand on it, twirl it around your wrist, feel its healing energy. Allow the bracelet to remind you to be more kind to yourself.

○ Identify your thoughts that were built upon the cruelty of old patterns and then construct something new from the foundation of *Wholeness (human divinity), Self-love, Play (the now moment)* or the *Embodiment of the Expanded Golden Rule.* Replace those thoughts with something like, "I am a divine sovereign being and I love me!" Imbed these new thoughts into the bracelet.

At first you may not believe the words; they may even be challenging to say and that's okay. Keep speaking them from a foundation of love, and you will begin to build the new neural pathways necessary to feel the divine truth of the statement.

Keep a journal of your new-thought bracelet experiences and note how your mental state shifts.

WELCOMING EACH EXPERIENCE

Positive mental wellbeing is not just the absence of mental illness. In his book, *Flourish*, Martin Seligman, the father of the field of positive psychology (the study of happiness) has this to say about wellbeing: "It is all too common-place not to be mentally ill but to be stuck and languishing in life. Positive mental health is a presence: the presence of positive emotion, the presence of engagement, the presence of meaning, the presence of good relationships and the presence of accomplishment. Being in a state of mental health is not merely being disorder free; rather it is the presence of flourishing."

Do you agree with Seligman's statements? Defining what mental wellbeing means to you is important, but *defining* is not the same as *knowing* how it feels inside you. Try the simple meditation on love in the next activity to get in touch with your own feelings of wellbeing.

Activity: Meditate on Love

(Do this as a group or by yourself.) Close your eyes, follow your breathing and focus on your breath for a few moments to find your center. Now, think about someone you love dearly and purely. This could be a family member, a friend or a precious animal in your life who is living or has already transitioned. Visualize him or her in your presence, right beside you, so happy to be near you. Focus on what they are wearing, how they smell and the smile on their face. Let yourself feel your love, so deeply. Open to the feeling. Once you anchor that love, feel its presence completely, let go of the image of the person or animal and focus entirely on the love itself. Be with it. Feel what happens in your heart and your body. This is a conversation with the spirit of what wellbeing is all about.

OUR OWN SACRED WITNESS

To us, wellbeing is attained through welcoming each experience, freed from the need to judge the experience. It means consistently making a deliberate choice to live each moment singularly without lumping what you are experiencing now into what you have previously experienced. There's a real grace to stepping back and learning to be our own sacred witness.

It's funny, but I (Kristy) started this chapter with a personal goal to do yoga everyday that I spent writing it. I felt a little stiff in my joints and I thought what a perfect gift to myself through this immersion into wellness. My body craved the gentle energy of the stretching. A healthy enough thought. But then my "story" crept in and my mind butted in. It said, "Yoga? That's not going to cut it. You need some serious cardio. Look at that muffin top!" So I ditched my original instinct, the request from my body, and pulled out the oldest, dustiest DVD from my cabinet, some torturous form of yoga dance fusion, not gentle at all, in order to placate my much louder mind. And man, did I get the message. After one crazy hour of this, my muscles rebelled so furiously I spent the next week nursing an injured, twisted up back. A pure example of how true wellbeing requires a synergy of all parts of us. Not strong-arming mind over body, but learning to listen to the entire conversation. The experience gave me a great opportunity to listen to my back for a week! And honestly, it had some important things to tell me, so I'm grateful for the dialogue. What I learned was that I had a story in my mind, a story which said that my mind knew better than my body, so I allowed judgment to override instinct. My body knew what it needed and my story butted in and caused me injury. I had temporarily fallen out of S.T.A.R. and blocked my own connection to my Fascinated Observer.

Our Story Is Our Choice

Being the Fascinated Observer means that we don't live imprisoned by the stories we tell ourselves. Our story is our choice. Our history just *is*. It's our choice whether we view our adversities from a place of "poor me" or whether we view our adversities from the vantage point of empowerment. The difference is, there's little real growth that takes place from spending our life within the victim's point of view. We want to be clear here, we're not saying that retreating to lick our wounds every now and then isn't a necessary and healing practice. But a chronic victim can be stuck in story, replaying the injustices over and over like a broken record, choosing to live in the past where the horrors originally took place. Or the flipside of that is choosing to live in the past where our so-called glories took place, seeing the perceived disappointments of our present reality through the eyes of the victim. Either way, we're not enjoying the bounty of this present moment.

From all over the world are stories of people who have risen from the ashes—from horribly brutal stories—to become fully-realized, self-actualized individuals using their past adversities to fuel a brand new incredible existence. We are here as humans to navigate these lives, riding the tides and managing the under-tow of these stories of ours, using each experience to sail to new shores. Experiences aren't black or white, they are all grey, in the purest sense.

> IN THIS MOMENT... WHAT PART OF YOU ARE YOU LISTENING TO?

Byron Katie, in her book, *Loving What Is,* has a beautiful example of this. She writes, "When I take people to the desert, they may see a tin can lying under a cactus and say, 'How can anyone do that to this beautiful desert?' But that tin can *is* the desert. It's what is. How can it be out of place? The cactus, the snakes, the scorpions, the sand, the can and us—all of it. That is nature, not a mental image of the desert without the can. Without any stress or judgment, I notice that I just pick up the can. Or I could tell the story that people are polluting the earth and that there is no end to human selfishness and greed and then pick up the can with all the sadness and anger I'd be feeling. Either way, when it's time for the can to move, I notice that I'm there, as nature, picking up the can. Who would I be without the uninvestigated story? Just happily picking up the can."

Katie has shown us an example of the Fascinated Observer in action: just picking up the cans strewn throughout our lives, without getting stuck in the sadness or the rage or the helplessness of any given situation. Are we focusing on what is wrong with our view? Or are we creating beauty with every opportunity we are given? From the eagle eye view of the Fascinated Observer, we live within the business of each passing moment without dragging the past or the future into it. Generally speaking, the sticky web of stories, the tossed-away cans of our spirit's landscape, reside in the experiences of our past or the anxieties of the future. We can take the same experiences of our past and see them through the lens of empowerment (what did we learn, how did we grow, what were the gifts of the experience) or we can choose to see them through the lens of disempowerment (I am forever broken, the world is a hostile place, I have lost my chance). *Who are we* choosing to be?

Buddhist psychotherapist, Jack Kornfield, in his book *The Wise Heart* asks the question, Who are we? Starting with the body we ask, "Am I the skin, the hair, the muscles and bones, the organs or the blood? Am I this body?" He goes on to remind us that biology teaches us that the molecules of the body are completely replaced every seven years. So, if we are not the physical elements of this body, then what are we? Are we the stream of changing feelings, he asks? Are we the memories and perceptions? Are we the thoughts and concepts, the views and beliefs? Who are we? The reminder here is that we are that which we choose to be. We can choose to identify with self-constructs that lead to entanglement and struggle or we can choose the path of dis-identifying (the Fascinated Observer) which may very well lead to freedom and ease. This is the heart of mental wellbeing: choosing where our mental processes, our thoughts, reside with every experience.

FINDING FASCINATION WITH HOT-BUTTON TOPICS

Can we play with some hot-button topics for a moment? What takes place in your mind when you hear "Monsanto" or "Fukushima" or the word "war?" Hot button subjects can cause a reaction where we unintentionally or intentionally send out an invocation for what we want. An unintentional invocation to "Fukushima" for example, might be to say something like, "Oh my God! We're all going to die of radiation poisoning because humans are war-mongering parasites filling the planet with the ingredients for nuclear disaster!" Doesn't exactly feel expansive, does it? In fact, it's such a scary way to conceptualize that it may just frighten a person into a complete state of non-action/complacency. What's the point? There's not much hope in that statement. The point is that we are feeding the fire with this energy, giving fuel to that which we do *not* want and fearing we are powerless to stop. The alternative is to approach it by changing how we think. Something like, "Humanity can now choose something precious and vitalizing. What choices can I *personally* make today that are healthy for the planet?" Can you feel your energy expand with this concept? It feels much more empowering and hopeful doesn't it? Can we effectively fight against wars with the same dark energy of the war? Gandhi didn't think so. Martin Luther King Jr. didn't think so. Neither does the Dalai Lama. We can run everything in life through the filter of objectivity and this is what the Fascinated Observer does. We give our energy to the quantum field infused with our earnest desires, which creates feelings of wellbeing.

I have a personal example of this. Recently, where Nina and I currently live in Santa Fe, New Mexico, an emaciated dog was found wandering. A heart-centered man walking his own dog stumbled upon the staggering four-legged skeleton at dusk. So exhausted, sick, starved and scared, the dog tried to snap at him when he reached to pet him, but he was so weak everything he did was in slow motion. The kind man still felt nothing but compassion for this being and somehow got him home to his warm house. He tried to offer him food or water, but the dog was beyond the desire for them, too starved to want to eat. In the morning, he brought the dog to the Santa Fe Animal Shelter. The shelter staff named the dog Raphael, after the archangel of healing and immediately began intensive veterinary work to ensure his survival. A picture of the dog circulated within social media and in no time it went viral. People all around the world were sending donations to the shelter in the name of Raphael. He was a miracle! Blood work showed no organ failure even though, with this severity of starvation, you would surely expect the kidneys or liver to cease functioning. The medical staff was optimistic. "He's going to make it!" they posted.

About this time, I came across the image of Raphael the starving dog and posted it on my own social media site. To me, the story was nothing short of miraculous. Here was this dog who against all odds was likely going to make it. And he was so loved. People all over the *world* loved him from afar, sending money and gifts for his wellbeing. His story was inspiring positive actions. I saw him as a diplomat, here to teach us more about the human-animal bond, more about an example to inspire our own compassion and caring. He was bringing awareness to animal welfare all over the world. His starvation and the rally which ensued to return his health to him, was a supreme sacrifice for the good of all domestic animals. It was as if he truly were Archangel Raphael, coming to earth in this incarnation to provide us a great inspiration.

And then I watched, with fascination, how many others didn't see it this way. People began to respond with black-magic perceptions; the stuff of mental anguish, not mental wellbeing. Anger, sadness, rage and horror…every comment was about retaliation against the people who did this to him or pity or severe depression over the plight of this poor animal and all animals like him. Focusing on the positive after positive details of this medical miracle was difficult for people because we have in the past been trained to look for what is wrong. Do we do this with our own lives too? It was so eye-opening for me to witness, because I have been that person in the past—the person who focuses on *what's wrong* rather than on *what's right* with the world and it has caused me much mental turmoil.

Many spiritual practices tell us, "This *should* be happening because it *is happening!*" in order to move beyond the old patterns of thinking such things like, "Cruelty shouldn't happen in the world!" Cruelty happens in the world. Radiation leaks happen in the world. Wars happen too. We are holographic beings, a mirror reflection of everything that has ever taken place in the history of our world and worlds beyond. When we own our divinity, our own place in all things horrible and beautiful, we can come to a place of fascination, which leads to transcendence. When we match the energy of war with war, more battles are created. What if events such as the Fukushima incident create the contrast to inspire or even force us through a disaster to transcend our current patterns?

We can use the S.T.A.R. philosophy on global issues that consume our mental wellbeing. For example, with Fukushima it looks something like this:

Surrender—We surrender the need to judge the creators and users of nuclear power. Our judgment, rage, sorrow, etc., will not eliminate the truth of disasters. We acknowledge our roles as divine sovereign beings to identify and find creative and wholesome means to power the need for energy to sustain our lives and the life of the planet.

Trust—We trust that, as divine sovereign beings, we chose to be part of this conundrum. In so owning our part, we can also experience the joy of creating a beautiful solution. We trust that we have the ability and the resources to do what *we* can to create and purchase power sources that are safe for and supportive to our planet.

Allow—We allow the answers to come. We put a new intention out into the quantum field and we allow a new solution to present itself. We imagine that those with the power to create wonderful new devices have the courage and means to follow through. We allow insight into the actions we are capable of implementing, as individuals, right now.

Receive—We receive the new insights needed to move forward into a place of innovation, so that healthy and beneficial forms of energy are created. We imagine us, as individuals, delightfully using this power.

And we bring in the Four Essential Qualities:

When we embrace the concept of *Wholeness (human divinity)*, we look at the metaphor it is expressing in our life. All is a metaphor; here it's about power and destruction. We bravely explore the difficult question of where in our life have we wrought destruction and craved power? It may look a lot different than the Fukushima meltdown, but owning our destructive qualities can cure our own meltdowns. We can use our distaste for Fukushima as an inspirational metaphor to explore where we are melting down or self-destructing.

When we embrace the concept of *Self-love*, we become the love. If we can explore our own part in all things across this holographic Universe and we can find total acceptance and love for ourselves, then we can find in our hearts to accept all that is, including Fukushima. This practice comes from a place of Oneness, and we can find peace by knowing we don't have to find the absolute answer for why this experience is occurring.

When we embrace the concept of *Play (the now moment)*, we understand that we can approach our problems from a place of mental wellbeing choosing to move into the octave of passion and joy/play within us. If we live moment-to-moment focusing not on our wrongs of the past but our visions for a new present, feeling in our bodies as if these visionary changes are already taking place—all is well. We maintain an openness to receive resolution, knowing that we may not have the solution to the earth's challenges, but we do have a divine intention to move forward in a way that brings more joy and wellbeing to the world.

When we embrace the concept of the *Embodiment of the Expanded Golden Rule*, we make conscious decisions to take actions based on what we feel is good and kind to every being on the planet, including ourselves. Depending upon what that might mean to us, we might choose to refrain from eating fish due to the radiation levels in the meat. Or we may stop eating fish to allow their numbers to recover from this stress. Or we may choose to begin studying the effects of nuclear power on the environment, knowing that in truth, our judgments have been influenced by the beliefs of other people rather than by facts. We may choose to offer blessings and prayers to those involved. Sometimes the best medicine for mental wellbeing is possessing the wisdom to take well-informed action.

Activity: Cool Down

This is a great exercise to work through any global issue that is causing you mental strain or stress.

We invite you to break down any issue that you are highly charged around into the S.T.A.R. formula (including the Four Essential Qualities). It may be something that's happening in the world today you wish to cool down.

Reformulate your stress by using the S.T.A.R. philosophy, spending as much time as you need doing so.

The challenge:

I Surrender:

I Trust That:

I Allow:

I Receive:

I Embrace Wholeness (human divinity):

I Embrace Self-love:

I Embrace Play (the now moment):

I Embrace the Expanded Golden Rule:

THE ATTENTION AND INTENTION OF MENTAL WELLBEING

Sometimes finding our own personal meaning of mental wellbeing requires both our loving *attention* and our sacred *intention*. We can focus our attention on where it is we have supreme control in our lives—our thoughts, our words, our personal actions—and form them into something lovingly directed at ourselves and those around us. We can focus our intention on those things which can cause us mental distress for which we feel we have no control. Our intention is a way of connecting with our personal divinity, which doesn't require the need for control. From there we understand our awesome role as creator beings on this planet. Nothing seems out of reach from this place of wholeness.

CHAPTER SEVEN:
MANAGING OUR EMOTIONS

OUR EMOTIONS GOVERN OUR EXPERIENCE. The S.T.A.R. philosophy is not about denial, and it's not about finding fault with ourselves either. We are spiritual beings having a human experience on earth. Our pain is inextricably connected to our humanity, as is our joy. It's not about exclaiming; "Everything's wonderful!" while remaining in an abusive relationship, pondering our recent traumatic car crash, going through a divorce or a financial crisis. We enter the pain in order to *merge with it* on our journey to transform it. This is an alchemical process of sorts requiring that we access the full range of feelings to turn that experience into "gold."

We humans are hardwired to feel. Our capacity for feeling is a divine gift. Feeling is the value in every experience. To keep an eye on our divinity doesn't mean we are to lose our humanity. We still need to navigate the pain *and* feel the pain when we're facing it, because if we can't, if we're too afraid, we lose our capacity to feel exuberance and joy as well. It's all connected, all wrapped up in the same repository. It was Kahlil Gibran who said, "The deeper that sorrow carves into your being, the more joy you can contain." Everything may not be wonderful, but everything is fascinating and everything is valuable when richness equals experience.

Activity: Journal of Triumph

Think back over your life to some of your most challenging memories. Now consider the following:

1. Which life event(s) shook you to your core and what did you do that helped you navigate your way through this difficulty?

2. Was there some action (or actions) that seemed to bring you healing, that made you stronger?

3. What enabled you to stand up and keep walking forward into the rest of your life?

Document every positive detail, your own journal of triumph, to remind you just how resilient you are. Keep adding to it, throughout your life, as you continue to gain strategies as a S.T.A.R. being. Refer to it when things become difficult. Humans are built to grow stronger from adversity. Remind yourself of this through this powerful exercise.

GOING BEYOND TRAUMA

Our emotional pain is critical in alerting us to an important connection that has failed or is frayed. Disconnection brings pain. When we disconnect from our divinity, our humanity, from our mindfulness, from our community of loved ones, from nature, we feel pain. Our emotional pain can be a reminder to connect with the Four Essential Qualities of *Wholeness (human divinity)*, *Self-love, Play (the now moment)* and the *Embodiment of the Expanded Golden Rule*. If, for example, we find ourselves in an abusive relationship, physically, emotionally, psychologically, whatever the abuse may be, how can connecting with the Four Essential Qualities assist us with where we are in this moment? There is no wrong answer here and certainly no easy solution. Perhaps the invitation is only to look at our current situation through a new lens. Understanding the magnitude of this topic—domestic violence has been properly labeled an epidemic—we want to tread with the utmost respect and love here.

When I (Kristy) was attempting to navigate out of my own past domestic traumas, I finally asked myself if I was accepting my own divinity. Was I? Was I connected to the *Embodiment of the Expanded Golden Rule?* Would I consciously treat others as I was allowing this treatment unto me? For me, the answer was no. And it was still incredibly difficult to walk out of that life into a brand new one where the loving man I ultimately found was waiting for me. But what brought me to that threshold was my near-sudden realization that I chose to not accept abuse. I didn't want it. I wanted to believe that I was here to be loved, honored, cherished and respected. My soul was ready for this new experience.

DO YOU BELIEVE IN YOUR OWN DIVINITY?

Arriving at self-love can sometimes require a long journey of healing, possibly utilizing psychologists, counselors, coaches or any number of healing modalities we are drawn to. Others have reported sudden spontaneous episodes of clarity, in which they describe an internal switch being flipped, instantaneously seeing their situation illuminated for what it is, without their painful complexes clouding their vision. There can be an episode of divine guidance in the form of a dream, a wild animal encounter or a few words from the lips of an angel disguised as a stranger. Either way, if we choose a new experience, we can find the path out of our destructive situation into a more loving life that is our divine right. That path may be long or short; who's to say but you? I found, in my own life, when I made my connection with the Four Essential Qualities, it became nearly impossible for me to remain in a situation incongruent with my soul. I chose to move on.

Transpersonal psychologists John Firman and Ann Gila write about a concept called transcendence-immanence in their book, *The Primal Wound*. They say, "Whether we are lifted to the heights of spiritual ecstasy or plunged into the depths of existential despair, we are distinct but not separate from (transcendent-immanent within) these experiences." In other words, we are *in* this traumatic experience but not *of* this traumatic experience. We can live our experiences without *becoming* our experiences. We can be in relationship with, but not identified with, anything we endure in human form.

"On the other hand," they go on to say, "when we become unwittingly identified with a particular content such as a belief, feeling or role, our entire experience of reality is conditioned by that particular content alone. Here we lose our sense of transcendence and become wholly immanent, enmeshed in the particular belief, feeling or role." We come to see the world through the lens of our identification. It becomes less about authentic feelings and more about addictions to neurotransmitters, programmed to prove and affirm our identity, our psyches reduced to searching for the next fix. Emotional wellbeing is influenced by our ability to become transcendent-immanent, and we do this by becoming the Fascinated Observers of our own lives.

The Fascinated Observer becomes adept at witnessing an experience without *becoming* or entangling their identity with the experience. It's the art of perfecting dis-identification with any experience. The Buddhists have been doing it for centuries, as have the Hindus and those in many other wisdom traditions. In so doing, we remain connected to our own divinity, our self-love, rather than finding identification with something external like an experience or an event.

The Beauty of Gray

Feeling connected is imperative to emotional wellbeing. It can be so tempting to ascend out of our humanity into the spirit realms and lose our footing on this planet. Seeking the totality of our being in both the darkness and the light, spiraling in the beauty of gray, helps us to get a grip on both our human experiences and our connection to Source. The pain and emotional stress may be intense. We are human and we have the gift of emotions. We are brilliantly hardwired for a vast array of emotions, not all dancing in the light. Every emotion is magnificent in its purest form, even the anger, the sadness, the confusion and the rage. Suppression or denial of any or all of the entire emotional spectrum can result in disharmony, sickness and sadness; an emptying of our disconnected heart. When our heart loses its ability to hold the vital energies of love and connection, nothing can keep it filled. We are left feeling empty and lost. It's okay to feel the emotions, all of them. They are the human experience.

Detach from Suffering from the Past

From *S.T.A.R. Philosophy* by Nina Brown (pages 94–99)

Years ago, I (Nina) met a man who suggested that I attend a three-day workshop sponsored by Landmark Education. I had no idea what the weekend conference he had suggested was about, but I trusted his recommendation. One evening before the event, the phone rang. The caller identified herself as staff for the Forum, the conference I was to attend. She wanted to know what I wanted to accomplish over the three-day period. What? No one had prepared me for that question, but I heard myself listing three things that I wished to resolve.

1. Peace with my deceased alcoholic mother

2. Peace with my cloistered Carmelite nun sister

3. Peace with my husband, whom I was divorcing

These were the three major events in my life causing me to experience emotional suffering from the past. At the time, I was engulfed with self-pity for all that I was enduring from each one of those relationships. There was no blueprint that I could find for a resolution. Without going into the details of what I believed each family member had "done to me," I now choose not to give power to the events by describing them as I used to remember them. The core issue with each situation stemmed from a perceived feeling of isolation, abandonment and ultimately lack of self-worth. It was easy to blame my mother, sister and husband for being the cause of those negative emotions.

My mother, Lanta, was an elegant Philadelphia lady who taught me graciousness and style. She was born into a middle-class family from a small town in Delaware. After she came to Philadelphia to study nursing, she met and married my father and quickly learned the fine qualities of proper society. Toward the end of her life, alcohol became her best friend, which also caused a shift in her personality.

My relationship with mother had always been strained, but it completely dissolved at the time of her death. I could not stand to look at an image of her, so the photos were packed in a box in my basement.

My sister, Alix, was my idol as I was growing up. Her love for me, her elegance and the fact that she was my only sibling caused me to want to show her off to all of my friends. She is four years older than me and has always held a special place in my heart, perhaps even more so because mother did not. When she went to study painting in Italy during her college years, she chose to convert her religious affiliation from being an Episcopalian to being a Catholic. Then shortly after her conversion, she traveled thirteen hours from her apartment in Florence, Italy, to San Giovanni Rotondo to attend mass with Padre Pio, a Capuchin Catholic priest, who is now venerated as a saint in the Catholic Church. While in prayer, she instantly knew that she wanted to choose a life as a consecrated religious. In her search for the order to join, she read a biography of St. Teresa of Avila and knew that she was to join the Carmelite order. She took her vow of poverty in June of 1964. I spent the next thirty years grieving the loss of my sister, Alix, who had transformed into the cloistered nun, Sister Pia of Christ Crucified.

My former husband, Grant, had a stellar career as a Philadelphia lawyer and was an expert in medical malpractice law defending doctors and hospitals. He loved to cook and arrange flowers, so he displayed both an academic and an artistic nature. He too found in alcohol relief from stress. After his second major episode, I asked for a divorce. The thought of how I was going to make a living did not enter into my thinking. I just knew that we could not continue as a married couple.

My mother, my sister and my husband were the focus of my weekend at the Forum, though they did not hold my full attention. The work that was presented to us was all-consuming and demanding. It called for a great deal of introspection in a very short period of time. The moment of my life-changing experience came when one of the instructors told me that "grief is words unspoken," and that those unspoken words were, "I love you."

I asked if one could speak the words to someone who was deceased and the answer was, "Yes."

I could hardly wait until the Sunday lunch break to tell my deceased mother that I loved her. How I was going to do that was not clear immediately. When the awaited time came, I went to the parking lot and got into my old car, a white Honda. Sitting quietly for a bit, it occurred to me to say the Lord's Prayer. Then I called on the spirit of my mother. Almost immediately, I felt her presence. My father was present as well. Out of my mouth came the simple words, "I love you." Then it occurred to me to kiss the etheric presence of my mother, which I did. A peace came over me, as I sat quietly in my car, until it was time to resume our work. When I drove home that evening after the completion of the weekend, I knew that my mother's spirit was with me. I immediately went down into the basement and retrieved a photograph of her that was in an old silver frame. I placed it prominently on a mahogany table, next to the couch in my living room.

The next day, Monday, I called Grant and asked if I could see him. Then I called the Carmelite Monastery and told the message machine that I would be coming to visit Sister Pia. Grant appeared at my doorstep soon afterwards. He did not choose to enter my townhouse, so we stayed on the front porch. I looked deeply into his eyes and said, "Grant, I need to tell you that I love you." The words or events that followed are not clear to me, but there was definitely a shift. It was as if any bitterness I had toward my husband slipped away.

When the day came that I was to visit Sister Pia, I was told to sit in the very sterile "speak room." My sister opened up the wooden screen that separated us. I could see her, behind the upright metal bars, dressed as usual in the brown and white clothing that she wore representing her order. Her skin was tight with no wrinkles and her cheeks, as always, were rosy and beautiful. Everyone who sees her goes away knowing that she is truly happy with the choice that she made at such a young age. I looked her in the eyes. "I love you" came easily out of my mouth. Then I gestured that I wanted to kiss her through the bars.

When we were complete, she said, "I have been waiting for you to tell me that." I left the convent in peace.

My goal had been accomplished, I was at peace with my mother, my husband and my sister, and it happened by means of changing my mind and speaking three short words, "I love you," to each one of my family members. The power that my emotional suffering had over me disappeared. Perhaps what occurred was a quantum leap. It felt as if the weight that had been on my shoulders had melted away. I was lighter and felt free.

The suffering I had known has never returned and I am in balance with all the people in my life because, with the wisdom of time, I have come to know that the way that a person expresses themselves through their personality, is not who they are. They too are divine humans.

At her essence, my mother was not a woman of society who drank to escape her loneliness. She was and is an enormous being of light who chose to experience incarnation under those conditions. My sister is not a devout, cloistered nun, whom I rarely see. She is an enormous being of light who chose to experience incarnation under those conditions. My now deceased ex-husband was not a successful attorney who chose scotch over his family and clients. He was and is an enormous being of light who chose to experience incarnation under those conditions.

The shift that occurred for me was experienced as a result of an intention or a choice. There was never an act of forgiveness, just love. There are currently few ties to the past that keep me from living my life in the now. My method of change or inner alchemy may not be yours. It matters not. What does matter is that we do the work, in whatever way is our path, into the now.

Phantom Emotions

Emotional wellbeing is dialoguing with and ultimately finding freedom from the emotional patterns which cripple us. Neuroscientists have found that when we re-live traumatic memories over and over, each episode of remembering causes the same physiological effects on our bodies as the actual event. Finding freedom isn't about denial, dissociation or disconnection from our humanness. It's about going directly into the pain to see where we can find our soul's evolution. It's going into the pain to see where we can find the humanity or even the divinity of the person or circumstance which delivered to us this painful experience, to see where we can find forgiveness for ourselves and others, if that feels right. No one can tell us how to "heal." We each have our own definition of the word and our own vision for what that might look like in our life.

Consider for a moment the possibility that the healing we're seeking doesn't even belong to us. Have you ever taken a moment to contemplate, as an empathic being, which emotional distresses belong to you and which ones you are lugging around for somebody else? To note the possibility of this, let's talk about something beyond fascinating called limbic regulation. As Jasmine Lee Cori writes in her book, *The Emotionally Absent Mother*, "In limbic regulation, one person's emotional brain entrains another's, whose emotional brain shifts to match the first person's. All mammals have this capacity, and it is thought to be a major mechanism through which an infant or young child's inner state is directly modulated by Mother. Just by gazing into the child's eyes, the mother communicates brain to brain with her child, bringing the child's limbic system into coherence with hers." This is beautiful when a mother is engaging with her child from a state of wholeness and balance, but imagine the lasting effects when she's not. When the mother is facing the struggles of mental illness herself, how many distressed children have simply been implanted with their mother's limbic programming?

Trauma and codependency author, Pia Mellody, believes that children absorb emotions from their abusers, carrying around the signatures of their oppressors far into adulthood. You can imagine how easily a child may accomplish this. Unable

CAN YOU TELL WHEN YOU ARE ABSORBING EMOTIONS?

HOW DO YOU KNOW IF THE EMOTIONS YOU EXPERIENCE ARE YOUR OWN?

to predict which behaviors will trigger punishment based on the chaotic nature of their care-givers, they learn to become highly sensitive, acutely reading their environments, psychically connecting with their abuser in an attempt to remain safe. Many of the world's most powerful empaths and intuitives credit their tumultuous childhoods as the training ground for developing their extraordinary gifts. In her book, *Facing Codependence*, Pia Mellody writes about what she refers to as *carried emotion*, which is carrying the induced feelings of others into adulthood, no longer having any clear sense of what belongs to you and what belongs to others. She writes, "One way to tell the difference between carried feelings and your own healthy ones is that carried feelings are overwhelming while your own, even though they may be intense, are not." In other words, somebody has a certain *tone* with us and it completely derails us, sending us into a cycle of toxic shame for a full twenty-four hours. When we can't figure out why we are so *destroyed* by a simple unkind word by a total stranger, it's likely we're carrying emotion around for somebody else. Perhaps it's our ancestral or familial signature. Do we choose to continue to carry around the emotional baggage of our entire lineage? If the answer is no, what do you sense is the first step for you to reclaim your energetic space, completely and purely?

We entrain to one another. We can stand two feet away from a complete stranger and feel their emotions without even having to look at their body language. A person seething with anger need not say a word for us to start feeling uncomfortable or fearful. If the person standing next to us is bubbling over with enthusiasm and excitement, those energies invade us too, often times giving us a jolt of energy more powerful than a double-shot espresso. A key ingredient to emotional wellbeing is the simple understanding that what we're feeling isn't always internally generated. It can be highly freeing to recognize that our emotions can get all jumbled up in another's. We have the ability to sort this out, to declare our physical, emotional and psychic boundaries.

It can be an important component of our healing to also recognize where we're inflicting our energy on others. When we hold a grudge, for example, we hold a part of a person's energy hostage. We psychically attach to them, through our thoughts and feelings. It hurts us, it hurts them. To have unhealthy attachments to another can feel invasive. Our unhealthy attachments may look very different from the extreme examples we see in the movies, but it can be important to evaluate to whom, if ever, have we or are we having unhealthy attachments? Our emotional wellbeing depends on being truthful with our self-evaluation. Sovereign beings have no need to place others on a proverbial pedestal. Sovereign beings recognize the complete equality of all beings.

Activity: Meditation for Retrieving Our Cords, Reclaiming Our Space

Without being conscious of it, we allow the energy reach of others, psychic tendrils if you will, to attach to our energy field just as we live within the energy fields of others without having any idea we're doing it. This meditation clears your space of inadvertent psychic intrusion and retrieves your own psychic reach from those you might be unknowingly draining. You are left feeling energized and whole as your space becomes the pure essence of you again. Do this as often as you like, to purify your field or protect your field should you find yourself in large crowds or anywhere else which may leave you feeling drained of your essence. (You may wish to record this meditation and listen to it while you close your eyes or you may wish to simply read through it and without worrying about the details, go through the "story" of it in your mind, knowing however it forms is perfect for you.)

Visualize yourself walking through a densely wooded ancient forest. The trees are so thick you can barely make your way through them.

Squeezing sideways between the trunks, stepping deliberately so as not to trip over heavy roots, you make progress forward.

Up ahead, you see light through all of this primordial darkness. You set an intention to reach the light and keep moving towards it. Moving, moving, you feel your progress as you finally reach the edge of a great round clearing.

Stepping through the dense undergrowth, you find yourself in a perfectly manicured circle of lush mosses, grasses and wild flowers.

You feel light and free in this natural expanse, beautiful and serene. You stop walking, the sun shining on your face, warm and soothing, to listen to the distant songbirds singing their elaborate, exquisite melodies. You are completely alone.

At this point you see a large flat stone, expansive enough to lie upon, a perfect granite platform. It seems a lovely place to take a rest and you walk to it, reaching it in a few short steps.

Sitting or lying down, relax on this great stone, the historian of your stories, experiences and secrets.

Feel the healing warmth of the sunrays soaking into your woodland throne. You lie here a moment and rest.

Before long you casually notice that your body sprouts roots which immediately enter the ground, coursing one hundred, one thousand, ten-thousand feet and beyond, down into the pulsing heart of Mother Earth.

You feel enormous love, the essence of the Divine Feminine as her energies course back up your roots finding a home in your magnificent human body, allowing you to retrieve every memory from this lifetime.

Bathing in this cool blue earth energy moving through your veins, notice now as individuals begin quietly peeking at you through the dense forest around you.

Family members, old lovers, friends you've moved on from... who shows up today? Perhaps you feel no recognition of them and that's okay too.

As they show up, ask them to release their energy from your field. Ask them to let go of you. Separate, with love.

Who remains attached to your field?

As you release each one, thank them and watch them walk away, back through the forest, into their own space. Feel free to be loving, but firm, if they resist detaching.

Allow them to each reveal themselves, one by one, until you have cleared your space entirely. This may take some time the first opportunity you have to practice this.

When this part feels complete, now, ask to see to whom you are attaching. Who are you resistant to releasing? Watch the forest as you pull them into your consciousness.

Watch these individuals, caught in your tractor-beam, arrive one by one, confused and dazed over why they're here. Why have you remained attached to their field? What is their connection to you? Are these connections born of love or trauma?

Tell them you release them to their own etheric field and let them go. Watch them sigh with contentment as they feel lighter, free to completely inhabit their own space again. We can remain in relation with someone without actually setting up home within their energy field.

Sense your energy as you are once again alone, breathing in freely and fully your own psychic signature.

As you lie here in purified earth energy bliss, you now feel the sun rays come alive to fortify you.

Reaching down from the sky, the dancing energy of the divine masculine enters you, fire energy igniting your senses, merging with the cool blue essence of feminine earth energy, creating a blinding light from within every cell, every capillary, vein, artery, illuminating you, a beacon of pure spirit. Bathe in this sensation, allow Mother Earth and Father Sun to clarify you, simultaneously grounding you and igniting you.

Now feel your roots retract from Mother Earth, feel the rays of Father Sun return to the cosmos knowing that they are forever connected to you, earth and sky.

As you feel your energy space completely cleaned out of anyone draining you, feel your own tendrils no longer needing to feed off of anyone else.

ALL PARTS OF US

When we claim our own space, from the place of our wholeness, no longer choosing to unwillingly live the experiences of those around us and no longer choosing to forcefully influence the experiences of others, we can receive emotional wellbeing as a kind of wondrous coming-together, a congruence of all parts of us that give divine meaning to our individual existence. Setting the intention to live from this place is a step toward releasing our unhealthy attachments to past memories or hurts. It's a step toward seeing others through the filter of sovereignty—you are divine, they are divine—rather than through the filter of emotional resentments, disappointments or grudges. When we fail to see our relationships through our divinity filter, we are also at risk for developing unhealthy attachments, addictions to people and the guru syndrome when we place all of our power within the hands of a teacher "more divine" than us.

Emotional wellbeing means we understand that we have the power to utilize any emotion as alchemical fuel for transformation. It means we have the endurance to experience any emotion without succumbing to it, though it may be crippling for as long as it needs to. There is no one recipe for alchemy; everyone has their own perfect process. We can accept that we have the power to transform. From there, we give our emotions the gift of freedom to express as they need appropriately.

CHAPTER EIGHT:
YOUR PRECIOUS BODY

AT THE TIME I (KRISTY) BEGAN WRITING THIS SECTION ON physical wellbeing, I had a ruptured ear drum from a severe cold and my dear friend's infant had just been diagnosed with tuberous sclerosis, a rare genetic disorder in which tuber-like benign tumors grow throughout the vital organs, most specifically the skin, the brain, the kidneys and the heart. An MRI had revealed that morning that the seizures the baby girl had been suffering were due to multiple tumors in her brain. Her father is a physician, her mother a health coach and yoga instructor, two of the most physically healthy people I know. Among all else that had been revealed that week through my body and the bodies of those close to me, this seemed like too much, until I heard the words from my friend, this baby girl's mother. She said, "This baby chose us. I love her more than anything. I trust her. I have to believe she knew what she was doing and that we can navigate this." This supremely graceful statement is about as pure a S.T.A.R. statement as I could ever write myself. It lifted me into a higher octave where I could rise up and experience it all from a place of love, not fear. It is unknown how difficult this baby's journey will be from here forward, and to be sure it will forever change the lives of her parents, but as her grandfather said in the hospital, "Love trumps all," and that is a truth we can't lose sight of. Physical wellbeing means more than seeking a symptom-free life.

Our physical bodies aren't something we were simply born to lug around, like baggage to dress and decorate. They are miraculous wonders, divine vessels and they have so much to tell us with every itch we scratch and every chill we feel. What is physical wellbeing but the ability to converse with our body, to learn from it in its infinite wisdom? We've been somewhat desensitized to the messages our bodies are trying to tell us and reliant on doctors to interpret the information. Doctors are necessary and helpful. The training we have received to numb the intimate messages (the symptoms) our bodies are communicating is not helpful in long-term soul-level healing. Within the full force of our physical conversations—our relationship to our body's discomfort—we experience what is *underneath* the symptoms, which often is a lot of emotional or spiritual pain. We silence our symptoms—rather than hear what they have to tell us—with pharmaceuticals or surgeries that can cure the physical symptoms but not the emotional distress at the source.

I (Kristy) was in the grocery store recently and in front of me was a woman buying a two-liter bottle of Coke, a package of frozen spicy burritos and a jumbo bag of "Red-Hot" spicy corn chips. Trailing behind on the conveyor belt was a family-sized box of heartburn medication. Now, who's to say who that heartburn medication was for and who's to say that she received any discomfort from eating these foods, if she was even the one eating them. But to me it felt like a metaphor and I noticed it. In that moment, I felt so sorry for all the poor tummies out there which try to talk to us through symptoms of heartburn and acid reflux, saying "No thank you!" to spicy foods, only to be silenced by pills. It struck me to look to see in my own life where I've masked symptoms rather than let them have their say, and it felt like a perfect example of *Self-love* to honor the voices of our body.

Activity: Sensing Nourishment

Visit three or four different grocery stores. Feel the energy of each place, jotting down details as you wander through.

- What are they selling?

- How does the food *feel* energetically?

- What's happening in your body as you wander the aisles?

- Pay particular attention to the produce section. Pick up the fruits and vegetables and hold them in your hands.

- Can you imagine the foods talking to you? Are they alive? Can you sense a buzzing, a lively frequency? What do you notice?

Ask your body, rather than listening to your mind, what it really craves when you walk into a place like this, filled with fresh and packaged foods. After visiting three or four establishments, compare your notes.

1. What have you learned through this exercise?

2. What insights has your body shared with you?

3. Journal your conclusions.

Our Body's Voice

Clarissa Pinkola Estes observes that "many people treat their bodies as if the body is a slave, or perhaps they even treat it well but demand it follow their wishes and whims as though it were a slave nonetheless." She continues to say that more importantly, a healthy dialogue with the body "is not what shape, what size, what color, what age, but does it feel, does it work as it is meant to, can we respond, do we feel a range, a spectrum of feelings? Is it afraid, paralyzed by fears, anesthetized by old trauma or does it have its own music, is it listening…is it looking with its many ways of seeing?"

Who are we to believe? Barraged by media campaigns, we see the benefit of eating all we want to eat, even if those foods make us sick, because all we have to do is take an H2 Blocker every day and voila! Our sickness is gone! We get to enjoy the spicy foods to our heart's content. But what if our constitution is not made for these types of foods and our heartburn is only one symptom they are causing us? Should we eat what we are not built for, which does not agree with us, only because there's a pill to remedy it? If our own body could control the media campaign what would it try to sell us? Likely it would be wholesome foods that we could use more powerfully than empty calories. Think about this for a moment! It's worth pondering. Can we learn to listen to our vital organs rather than silence them?

Years ago when I (Kristy) was nearing the end of my career in veterinary medicine, my body was literally screaming at me to make tremendous life changes or suffer the consequences. I had blood pressure so high it could barely be controlled with a cocktail of three different anti-hypertensives. My anxiety was through the roof, so I took pills for that. I was depressed because I wasn't finding fulfillment in my work or my life, so I took pills for that too. I had an ulcer, I had migraines and I had a bizarre croupy cough that no amount of inhalers or asthma medications could clear up. I had medical exams of my lungs due to the strange cough, but nothing was clearly diagnosed and no relief could be found. I was seeing a psychologist and a psychiatrist, and though my body was screaming—TRY SOMETHING NEW!—no one suggested my lifestyle was the issue. It didn't make sense. I was successful, looked good, was thin and well-dressed, drove a nice car…I just kept getting more and more prescriptions thrown at me and escorted out the door with a smile and a pat on the back. One day my psychiatrist actually said, "Go get 'em tiger!" as he tucked another anti-depressant sample in my pocket.

So one day I woke up and left my job, gave my notice and walked away from a twenty-year career. I was simply being called to express in a completely new way. I was asking to transcend the material realm and live my life at a higher octave, driven by heart and spirit. All along my body was trying to alert me to this new imperative evolution, but I was afraid to listen. Even after a trip to the emergency room with a hypertensive crisis of blood pressure of 210/140 (the stuff of strokes), I was still too afraid to make the monumental life change I was destined to make. But I finally did it. And though there's a lot to the story, the short version is my soul took the driver's seat, my divine purpose revealed itself and within two months of leaving the past behind to begin something new, I was symptom free and off every medication. No more hypertension, no more anxiety, no more OCD (obsessive compulsive disorder) that I had struggled with my entire life, no more headaches and most incredible, no more cough that had followed me around for a decade. My body just relaxed, sighed, flopped in a chair and said, "THANK GOD she finally listened!" Without a single doubt, had I not chosen a new course, I believe my body would have exhausted itself with all its S.O.S. signals. I believe I would have died an early death, possibly following in the footsteps of my mother who died in her late forties.

Today, my body still talks. It still throws out S.O.S. signals when it needs to have a conversation with me. Each signal is new and has something novel to say, but today I know how to listen. It's no longer my first instinct to run to the pharmacy to suppress my body's voices. I stay with the symptom until I have an understanding of its underlying message and by going deeply into it, by listening intently, oftentimes my body's voices become quiet. I still see the doctor and take pharmaceuticals when I feel it's indicated. But I understand that like any other living organism—every system in our body is a living organism—there is contentment in being seen and heard. I used to silence my pain with pills, without having that conversation first. Billions of us still do. In my own life I have found value in my physical pain because it alerts me that a new way of doing things may be indicated. Our bodies have a wide range of sensations, just as our emotions have their own wide range. When we feel sadness or anger or anxiety, it's often an invitation for us to look deeper into our being. The same invitations can be found through our physical mumbles and grumbles.

> WHAT ARE YOU BEING CALLED TO EXPRESS IN A DIFFERENT WAY?

BREAKING NEW GROUND

With sickness comes choice. Would we like to restore our health to the state it was prior to the illness? Or would we like to use this illness as fuel, possibly achieving a new state of wellness never reached prior to the physical challenge? We hear about these inspiring stories all the time. A man has a heart attack and comes through with a new devotion to wellness. He runs a marathon a year later. A woman survives cancer and comes through it with a new purpose, devoting her life to educating others about holistic nutrition. A man is diagnosed with Crohn's disease and comes through it with a new devotion to his physical wellbeing, becomes more fit than he's ever been, crediting the disease as his inspiration. Our bodies are capable of incredible regeneration! And the science of epigenetics (which means literally "control above genetics") tells us that our destiny is much more complex than the sum of our genes. Dr. Bruce Lipton, in his classic book, *The Biology of Belief*, writes, "In the last decade, epigenetic research has established that DNA blueprints are not destiny! Environmental influences, including nutrition, stress and emotions, can modify those genes without changing their basic blueprint." This means we, the divine beings that we are, can control our own destiny. Changing our thoughts can actually alter how our brain communicates with our body, changing our system's biochemistry entirely. Isn't this incredible?

There is no greater example of this than the power of the placebo (which is Latin for "I shall please"). The concept of the placebo has confounded the medical industry for decades, but it's nothing short of miraculous. The placebo effect is when we're given a sugar pill or a saline injection (for example) with absolutely no medicinal qualities and because we believe we're receiving outside assistance from the pill and from the doctor, we cure our self. There are countless examples of this in the medical literature and entire institutions like Harvard's Program in Placebo Studies and the Therapeutic Encounter have been dedicated to understanding this phenomenon.

Considered to be even more powerful is the nocebo effect (which is Latin for "I shall harm"). The nocebo effect happens when we believe that harm will befall us and it does. Science attributes the power of "voodoo" curses to this nocebo effect. Some examples peppered through the medical literature include:

○ Patients in a control group study were injected with saline, warned it could be chemotherapy and thirty percent of the group lost their hair.

○ People were given a drink of sugar water, warned that they could become nauseous as a result and eighty percent of them vomited.

○ Study participants were told that the nitrous oxide (actually something that *alleviates* pain) delivered to them may cause them pain and it did.

There is no definitive medical explanation for why people get better with placebo or worse with nocebo, but what is clear is that our minds are capable of healing our physical bodies or harming them. What if we declared from this moment forward that our minds will be used for the sake of wellness only? No more using nocebo as a weapon against our bodies? As divine sovereign beings we understand this to be a choice.

Lissa Rankin devotes her life to helping us understand this truth. A physician, speaker and writer, she's leading her own revolution toward a new understanding of our concept of physical wellbeing. In her book, *Mind Over Medicine*, she describes her own medical intake form for her patients, which looks different from any other form I've ever seen in a doctor's office. She asks these questions, "Is anything keeping you from being the most authentic, vital you? If so, what is holding you back? What do you love and celebrate about yourself? What's missing from your life? What do you appreciate about your life? Are you in a romantic relationship? If so, are you happy? If not, do you wish you were?"

She goes on to ask, "Are you fulfilled at work? Do you feel like you're in touch with your life purpose? Do you feel sexually satisfied, either with a partner or by yourself? Do you express yourself creatively? If so, how? If not, do you feel creatively thwarted, like there's something within you dying to come out? Do you feel financially healthy or is money a stressor in your life? If your fairy godmother could change one thing about your life, what would you wish for?"

When asked what they believe lies at the root of their physical illness, her patients responded with answers like,

○ I give until I'm depleted.

○ I'm miserable in my marriage.

○ I absolutely hate my job.

○ I need more "me" time.

○ I'm so lonely I cry myself to sleep every night.

○ I'm out of touch with my life purpose.

○ I don't feel God anymore.

Our physical symptoms extend far beyond our bodies into the lives we are living on a daily basis. Our physical bodies are finely-tuned instruments, radars, to alert us when we're heading down a path that isn't aligned with our wholeness. Physical illnesses and their symptoms are here to have dialogue with us; indeed they can be our greatest gifts. Their effects on us are only a story away from helping us or harming us and we're the storytellers of our own life.

And yet, when sad things happen, it is our instinct to spend most of our time wondering why. When illness descends upon us or upon our family, the first question is why? Why do "bad things happen to good people?" We've heard that question hundreds of times across the span of our lives, in various contexts. It's easy to fall into the pattern of answering this question for others around us. "Obviously this happened to them because…" Or even telling a person, to their face, something like, "You were in the car accident because you needed to feel the lesson of non-control."

Let's take this moment to explain the S.T.A.R. philosophy while reviewing this:

We are divine sovereign beings. That means only WE can answer those questions on behalf of our own body and our own life. We may choose to seek counsel of others, specifically by asking another what their take on our situation is, perhaps even paying them to do so. But even that is entirely our call. It is not up to us to declare an uninvited teaching for another based on communication from *their* body. Understanding the power of the nocebo, we understand that *it can be detrimental to do so* and oftentimes when we have the urge to assign a reason for another's challenges, it's only our projections based on our own experiences that we're speaking. Our truth doesn't necessarily equal another's and could actually cause harm, which is the opposite of the *Embodiment of the Expanded Golden Rule.*

HOW WOULD YOU WRITE YOUR NEW STORY?

A great example of this is my mother's words on her deathbed. I (Kristy) so wanted her to heal herself. But my version of Mom healing herself was rising from her hospital bed cancer-free and better than ever. Her version of healing was something very different. Realizing she only had hours left, I went into a state of panic. With my mother showing a rare window of lucidity, I took the opportunity to tell her that I didn't want her to die. I said through my tears, "So you're just going to give up? You're just going to let the cancer win?" I was only nineteen years old and terrified of the thought of losing her. With the calm of a Zen monk, she smiled and held my hand. She said, "Winning to me means full acceptance of this moment, whatever that may bring. I am at peace with my death. Don't you see? I *have won.* I'm not afraid." She died twenty-four hours later and her words have been with me every moment since. To me, her S.T.A.R. statement revealed to me the mastery of physical wellbeing. We can die healed, even if we aren't cured. Only our soul knows the whys of our lifetime.

THE SENSUOUS BODY

Improving physical wellbeing calls for a refined level of intimacy with our own bodies. Using all of our senses, we come to connect with what our pain means, what our body wants for nourishment and how it wishes to move and play. We learn to speak with it, as we come to recognize that every cell holds its own sovereign consciousness, an entire Universe inside of us. From this moment, we ask you to declare your love for your body. Recognize it as the most divine physical temple. Then ask it, "Where do we go from here?" Is your body asking anything of you? Physical wellbeing invites this conversation. Ask the questions and see what part of your body chimes in. Fascination, guaranteed.

Your body is a walking miracle; a physical manifestation of the Universe you're creating for yourself. Perhaps you recognize this. But if you don't, what would it take to begin the journey of believing it?

CHAPTER NINE:
THE SPIRITUAL JUNCTION

WHAT IS SPIRITUALITY? To us, this is what connects us to our wholeness, our expanded beautiful self. Our wholeness can be defined as something we call the *junction point*, that place where our humanness and our divinity merge. If our spiritual life could be seen as an hourglass, the junction point would be where life happens, where the sand pours through, our life-blood, where we both own our divinity and claim our humanity, with all of its messiness and glorious beauty. From that place of wholeness we align with the Four Essential Qualities: *Wholeness (human divinity)*, *Self-love*, *Play (the now moment)* and the *Embodiment of the Expanded Golden Rule*. A merging of these elements brings us a sense of spiritual wellbeing, a critical component to a life well lived.

Dr. Gerald G. May, a psychiatrist who studies the sixteenth-century writings of John of the Cross and Teresa of Avila, writes in his book, *The Dark Night of the Soul*, that according to John and Teresa, "the human mind can never grasp the real truth of God; it is always beyond us. Any conclusion or image we come to about God, no matter how wise, will always remain incomplete. Thus there can be no clear right and wrong about how one perceives one's own relationship with the Divine. 'God and me' has its truth, as does 'God in me' and even 'God as me.' Any of these taken by itself, however, leads to distortion. And even taken all together, they still are incomplete." This is a great summary of the complexity of the human spirit and how we choose to see God. In us, as us, outside of us or all of the above, the S.T.A.R. philosophy orbits around the central sun of owning our own divinity. We are each a ray of that central sun, Source energy, uniquely expressing in our human forms.

I (Nina) have at times been struck with the existential pain of this "earthbound" human existence, until I entered that sadness completely. Entering the pain under the pain, I found the foundation of it was upheld by my own separation from Source. Ascending into the etheric realms so completely resulted in a disconnection from my human expression. I lost my place within the junction point and thus when I lost my humanity I also lost my connection to my wholeness. I learned that being in the trenches with my humanity, so to speak, was a critical piece to my own divinity. And conversely speaking, when we lose our connection to our divinity, a dark night of the soul ensues and causes us equal pain and sadness. We have heard many stories of those experiencing this very thing, in their own words and their own expression, a common human thread. We are all together in this Oneness.

It's important to remember this because sometimes in our passion, we lose sight of another's belief. We forget that we're looking at a mirror image of our self, another ray of Source energy, expressing in their unique way, wearing whatever costume their soul chose to gather experience in this incredible Universe. There are over seven billion people living on this planet earth. What are the chances we're all going to think *exactly* alike and share identical beliefs? There are those who believe very differently than we do, and to those people we say, "We honor you and your beliefs." Our passions are beautiful until they are misdirected and used to make another person wrong. Our passions can easily become weapons when that becomes our truth. Few people will argue that Mahatma Gandhi initiated great change in this world. He said this about misdirected passions, "It is quite proper to resist and attack a system, but to resist and attack its author is tantamount to resisting and attacking oneself. For we are all tarred with the same brush and are children of one and the same Creator, and as such the divine powers within us are infinite. To slight a single human being is to slight those divine powers and thus to harm not only that being but with him the whole world." A powerful message.

Activity: Detox Negative Energy

It's not unusual for us empathic human beings to absorb external energy that doesn't feel good to us. You might feel heavy or dense after visiting a large fair or public place with hundreds of other people. Since we're all swimming together in one big psychic soup, it's possible to pick up fragments of the frequencies of others, which may feel foreign to your unique energy field. Occasionally this calls for a defragmentation of our own system! Try this and see if you feel differently once you're finished.

- Focus on your breath, meditate for a few minutes or find a beautiful spot outside in your garden to center yourself.

- Use your breath to draw in your vitality, your unique life-force frequency. With each inhalation, draw in the pure crystalline energy of your divine blueprint.

- Visualize retrieving every drop of your energy you have recently lost. Keep inhaling until you feel complete. Feel the energy flowing through your cells, your capillaries, your vessels and vital organs. See it as a sparkly cleansing, permeating and purifying your entire energy field.

- Exhale any negative energy you're holding onto, any energy that doesn't belong to you.

- Visualize all the external energy garbage that doesn't belong to you exiting your field. Feel yourself becoming lighter, with each exhalation cleaning your energy field.

- Bathe yourself in cleansing sunlight or take a sea-salt and essential oil bath to stabilize your ions into a place of harmony. Feel your energy field sparkly fresh and entirely you.

Do this as often as you need to when you feel you're carrying around external energy that doesn't belong to you.

Do you remember a time when you sensed you were carting around some-body else's energy? What did it feel like to you? How did you ultimately clear your energy field? Take a moment to comtemplate your answers.

Say What?

Recently Nina experienced her first insulting remark on the internet. It seems we've all been indoctrinated into the new world order where it seems to be that *anything goes* on social media sites. It's an incredible tool for strengthening our mental and spiritual reserves. She wrote a few words and someone responded in strong disagreement. Her initial reaction was a jolt of pain. "I must have said or done something wrong!" she immediately processed. And then instantaneously her own human divinity and self-love kicked in. She hadn't done or said anything wrong. She expressed herself and somebody expressed himself in return. Nobody was right or wrong. She didn't need to choose to internalize his anger. She made another choice. And then she appreciated this man for revealing to her an important piece of her own development. A person doesn't have to share our spiritual beliefs for them to remain sacred. When we fully own our spiritual expression, we are a living embodiment of them. We become the Fascinated Observer of the beliefs of others. Their divergence proves no threat to our foundation just as ours proves no threat to theirs. We can choose a no-drama zone where it pertains to our own spirituality. Nina writes in *S.T.A.R. Philosophy*, "Being in a state of no drama in this instance suggests equilibrium of emotions, a state in which we no longer overreact to or exaggerate the importance of events. What is, is. The events simply are. Our new wisdom, which has no emotional spark, allows us to be or not to be the observer of events, without identifying with them or getting a chemical 'high' from them."

I (Kristy) used to have a hard time with this. I was born with no shortage of fiery passion and that fire always ignited around spirituality. I blamed it on my Catholic upbringing; I left the church when I was eighteen. At the time, when anyone else would point out that the beliefs of others were wrong, I would go ballistic! Once my priest delivered a sermon in which he declared Buddhists nice people, which he said was really too bad, because they were all going to hell. I walked out. Only fourteen years old at the time, but I just couldn't stomach it. I thought it was horrible what he said! But the way I dealt with my truth was to point a finger and judge the "wrongness" of another individual, which was exactly what I was rallying against! I could have remained in my power, feeling secure in my own beliefs and had an honest conversation with this priest after the mass, sovereign being to sovereign being. At fourteen, this may have taken some nerve. But simply shouting "Wrong!" and running away…well, I may as well have just carried a mirror around with me, gazing at my own reflection through my tirades! It was all so ridiculously humorous. I wish I could say I was all grown up and evolved from this tendency by the age of fifteen, but in truth it can take awhile to see where we're getting stuck.

WHERE DO OUR BELIEFS COME FROM?

Of course when we respond with rage when a person challenges our belief systems, spiritual or otherwise, the foundation of the anger is generally pain and fear. If we have a tentative grip on our beliefs and feel that the challenges of others are capable of annihilating our beliefs or our very existence, we are faced with the terror of non-being. It's painful to be told we're wrong. And let's face it, in all of our histories are stories of our ancestors literally being killed for having beliefs that differed from those of the stronger or more powerful. But Jack Kornfield in his book, *The Wise Heart*, shows us another way. He writes, "In a healthy response to pain and fear, we establish awareness before it becomes anger. We can train ourselves to notice the gap between the moments of sense experience and the subsequent response. Because of the particle-like nature of consciousness, we can enter the space between instinct and action, between impulse and reaction. To do so we must learn to tolerate our pain and fear. This is not easy."

The journey to tolerate my pain and fear was for me a complex undertaking that took an incredible amount of inner work to assimilate. And to me, seeing the divine in others, especially those with very different beliefs, is a spiritual practice in and of itself. It can be painful, because it requires a large amount of what is referred to as *shadow* work, which is identifying those parts of us we don't like to see or admit. Integrating our shadows means not only identifying those aspects of us but loving and embracing them as great divine gifts. When we can do this with our own being, we can learn to do it with others, and there we find spiritual freedom. In his book, *Integral Spirituality*, psychologist Ken Wilber says, "Enlightenment is being one with—or transcending and including—all states and all stages at any given time in history." This means, becoming it all, owning it all. What we can't own becomes our shadow. What Debbie Ford, author and coach, frequently said about that is, "What we don't own, owns us." All so fascinating. Spiritual freedom means spiritual acceptance of all spiritual differences.

LIVING FROM THE JUNCTION POINT

The philosophy of *Surrender, Trust, Allow, Receive* along with the Four Essential Qualities of *Wholeness (human divinity)*, *Self-love*, *Play (the now moment)* and the *Embodiment of the Expanded Golden Rule* is a pathway to liberation from that which has in the past hindered us. This could be seen as a process that ultimately leads to reaching our divine purpose

HOW DOES THE SOUL LEAD THE HUMAN

and/or potential. When we reach that octave, we establish connection to our junction point, that place where our divinity and our humanness merge. We feel something different from that which we had felt in the past. Comparison loses power. We don't identify with praise or insults. Liberation comes when we consistently practice our skills as the Fascinated Observer. Spiritual wellbeing is what results when this takes form. Deepak Chopra affirms this in *The Spon-*

taneous Fulfillment of Desire, when he says, "If we could learn to live from the level of the soul, we would see that the best, most luminous part of ourselves is connected to all the rhythms of the Universe. We would truly know ourselves as the miracle-makers we are capable of being. We would lose fear and longing and hatred and anxiety and hesitation. Living from the level of the soul means diving past the ego, past the limitations of the mind that harness us to events and outcomes in the physical world."

So, if you're living a S.T.A.R. existence, you understand that there is no right or wrong way to be spiritual. Your soul leads you, guides you, to that numinous pathway toward your own wholeness, the junction point between your own divinity and your own humanity. What words you choose make no difference; whether you call it meditation, contemplation or prayer, it's the ritual you choose that matters, based on your own internal guidance. Spirituality is not waiting for an external force to tell you what is right or wrong, good or bad or any other message delivered to tell you that you're dependent upon a source outside of yourself to claim your own divinity. When I was about twelve, my catechism teacher told us we should put tacks in our shoe and walk around all day feeling the pain, in order to sacrifice our comfort for Jesus. I loved my catechism teacher, she was wonderful, but my own internal guidance told me this advice was off. When I connected to my soul, I felt that Jesus would actually be sad if I did that, not happy. So I said no thanks and the teacher suggested perhaps a small rock instead. Nope. That didn't feel right either. I have always been pretty tight with Jesus and he wasn't telling me to do such things. For me, spirituality wasn't about choosing pain. It was about choosing joy.

Wrapping It Up

What is wellbeing? To us, wellbeing is a coming together, a harmonious exchange between all of the components of our interior and exterior being. It's the junction point, where all roads meet. It's a synergy that takes place, a conversation we have with our entire being, a dialogue born of acceptance and love and feeling and grace.

It's all of it—the good, the painful, the beautiful, the ugly. It's what naturally happens when we stop exiling parts of ourself because we judge them to be wrong or bad or worthless.

Wellbeing is an understanding that whatever shows up, we can work with, if only our foundation is built from a place of *Wholeness (human divinity)*, *Self-love*, *Play (the now moment)* and the *Embodiment of the Expanded Golden Rule*. Wellbeing is allowance. It's the allowance of our life to unfold, understanding the full range of our miraculous powers, knowing that whatever crosses our path, we will handle it. We chose that experience and we can choose the next one. Set the intention to live from your junction point and you'll start a new journey to wellbeing.

PART FOUR:
PLAYFULLY FASCINATED

How Do We Get to NOW?

From *S.T.A.R. Philosophy* by Nina Brown (page 90)

Now is play. When I give this special definition, people often look quite puzzled. To play is to be in the now moment of no time/no space. Have you ever asked yourself, "What does 'to play' mean?" What does it mean when my grandson says to me, "I want to go out and play?" Play what? He is not referring to soccer or cards. He just wants to play.

On reflection, over many months of asking for the definition of play, it came to me that play is defined as: being in the now. So, what does play look like for adults when they are not actively involved in a game of play? Can we be playing while sitting on the porch looking at our flowers? Can we be at play when we are visiting a friend, shopping, at the bank or working at our job?

The answer is yes, on all of those occasions we can be in the now, being completely engaged in the creativity of the moment with no attachments, memories or patterns from the past controlling our thoughts. We can be so immersed in the flow of the moment, outside of our environment, our personality and time that we connect with the quantum (discrete energy) field of all possibilities, from which we can choose new thoughts or their resulting experience with joy and appreciation, the feeling of play.

CHAPTER TEN:
THE ADVANCED CONCEPT OF PLAY

WHO KNEW THE CONCEPT OF PLAY COULD so thoroughly kick my butt? As I (Kristy) began this section, my initial enthusiasm for the material quickly underwent an evolution into pure resistance. "I can't write this!" I argued. Grappling with the idea of handing the whole thing off for Nina to finish, forces within me ignited to give me the tools to examine what was happening internally. Why was I so afraid of Play? After entering a complete stall, giving myself permission to go into an energetic "coma," as a dream had guided me to do, I found a core piece of me that seemed to be the heart of this section. Permission...when do we stop *granting ourselves the permission* for pure play with the freedom that children so naturally embody? Like President Business in *The Lego Movie*, I understood that my play was generally *conducted* with a logical purpose. How sad! I was attaching analytical meaning to it. I'd make room to be more creative so my work could expand, or I'd plan to rejuvenate my spirit for "x" amount of days. Play was something to cross off my to-do list! It was never done for the sake of the play itself. And I realized that though I constantly espoused the idea that play is imperative, I didn't know how to give myself to it with no expectation. Play, for play's sake alone, is a difficult concept to surrender to, for me and many like me.

When we play openly and freely, we enter the realm of timelessness. We open to the home of the Fascinated Observer. There is a term coined by a happiness researcher, positive psychologist Mihaly Csikszentmihalyi, called *flow*. Flow streams when we find ourselves in that place of timelessness, when we are so engrossed in our play (which can look an awful lot like work when we love what we're doing) that glancing at the clock sends shock waves through us. Four hours have passed? Impossible! We only just sat down, what seems like moments ago and suddenly the sun is setting and we're not in the least bit tired. Kids are experts at this, right? What would it look like in our lives if flow were an active player? How would our life shift if we regularly entered this place of timelessness, the realm of the Fascinated Observer, just loving the moments without judging the necessity or the practicality or the logic of our actions? Daniel Pink writes in his book, *A Whole New Mind: Why Right-brainers Will Rule the Future*, "Like its five sibling senses, Play is emerging from the shadows of frivolousness and assuming a place in the spotlight. *Homo ludens* (Man the Player) is proving to be as effective as Homo sapiens (Man the Knower) in getting the job done."

IF YOU, THEN YOU

Think about the context of the words "If you, then you," and explore the energy behind them. Do you recognize the formula? In my own life it has sounded something like, "*If I* eat this cupcake after dinner, *then I* will have to skip breakfast tomorrow." That's really no fun. A cupcake every now and then doesn't have to mean deprivation the next day. This is an invitation to start implementing the *if you, then you* in a rewarding context, rather than a punishing form.

Journal about the following four questions:

- What do you believe play is?

- How do you feel when you don't get any time for play?

- Do you punish yourself for playing too hard?

- What do you have to accomplish to deserve play time?

Let your creative energies flow through the questions and let this be an invitation to add play into your weekly (or daily!) routine. Change the context of the *if you, then you* to pure rewarding behavior. "*If I* write for five hours today, *then I* get to stop everything and take the dogs to the park." It's so easy to flow from work to more work to more work still! This is an exercise in setting the intention to play.

We know the importance of intention, so this left me wondering, how often do I play and not completely allow its medicine to enter me for lack of recognizing my own intention for the time spent? We unceremoniously go to dinner with friends, because that's what we do on Saturday nights. We have a great time, but do we fully open to the timelessness? Do we check our watches, thinking about everything we have to accomplish tomorrow before going back to work on Monday? Children naturally embody the spirit of play through the ingredients of storytelling, imagination, mimicking, role-playing, pretending... all of the things we do as adults on a regular basis and just don't recognize as play! So this left me wondering, how much is the concept of play a kind of quantum jump into a parallel existence in our own life? Is there an invitation here to simply see ourselves as creatures who play—who *choose to play* for its supreme importance, as the only logic necessary to justify it?

> DO YOU BELIEVE IN THE POWER OF PLAY?

This triggered a visual of a memory I had years ago. I have always been a highly structured person. My friends laugh at the memory of me as a twenty-one year old, sitting by myself in my spotlessly clean apartment, passing up invitations to go to the bars on a Friday night because I was so engrossed in a project I was working on, which was memorizing all the major rivers in the world. Yes, you heard me correctly. Rivers. I craved order. As a child of a chaotic family of alcoholism and addiction, my only medicine was to become so controlling and structured that nothing could surprise me. Surprises meant that horrifying monsters could leap out of the nearest closet. I once outlined a twelve-hundred page book on World War II in my desire to make order out of chaos. I truly love structure!

So that counteracting memory, which my contemplation of joy and play as supreme importance triggered, was life changing for me. It happened in my mid-twenties. I was in Hawaii vacationing. My boyfriend and I were lounging on a small boat we had rented. Anchored out in the bay, we were soaking up the sun, staring at the placid deep blue waters, deeply restful and contemplative. Suddenly and without warning, the quiet sea exploded around us in every direction like bombs detonating; it felt like missiles were launching and landing just a few feet from every deck. My immediate terror turned to the cascading adrenaline of joy in less than a second of cognitive processing. Spinner dolphins!

They were everywhere! Leaping ten feet into the air, spinning like dancers, whistling, pirouetting in twos and threes, a perfect show they orchestrated. It seemed they purposefully chose us as their audience, and their performance lasted a full five minutes or more. I lost time. I could barely breathe I was laughing so hard. I was standing and clapping and screaming and pointing and trying to take pictures of this magnificent and powerfully potent display of pure chaos. My international businessman boyfriend, no stranger to structure, a man who wore tasseled dress shoes to mow the lawn, became equally ecstatic, laughing until his stomach hurt. What a moment that was for us! The JOY of chaos! Is this what play is, in this context?

Dolphins have long been a totem of joy, play and fun; they are teachers for us in so many ways. Can they remind us to make that quantum leap into being more playful creatures? Nina visualized her version of this: The Golden Dolphins, years ago when they told her that we might follow in their wake, learned to use them as models for our transition into the S.T.A.R. philosophy. It was through their energy that she also learned of the Four Essential Qualities. Scientists can give us all kinds of theories as to why spinner dolphins spin— they're dislodging parasites, they're increasing their capacity for digestion, they're communicating great hunting spots—and these may all be valid. But for anyone who's watched them, up close and personal, hurling themselves out of the water with impossible torque, spinning sometimes up to seven complete rotations in the air, you can almost feel them clapping for each other. It's a celebration to a person witnessing it, a display nothing short of magical. Marine biologist Richard Connor in his book, *The Lives of Whales and Dolphins*, tells us that many species of dolphin possess the largest brains in relation to body size in any nonhuman animal. They are thought to be the most intelligent of all creatures in the animal kingdom. Some say they're more intelligent than humankind. With all of this cognitive capacity, they are also some of the most playful creatures on the planet. Their lives are full of very real dangers, most of them delivered by our species. And through it all, still they play, they charm, they delight, they change people's lives like they did mine so many years ago.

Activity: From Serious to Silly in 60 Seconds

My dog is a master at silly. She has this habit of throwing around her food bowl if it's empty, picking up her water dish and literally throwing it into the room we're occupying if we should become lax in our duty to keep it filled and fresh. She also throws toys at us if she wants us to play. I love the message in that. Toys to her are as important as food and water; a staple need in her life! What a lesson in that for us! Dogs are fun fanatics. We could learn a thing or two from dogs.

Your mission for play: For one week, observe silly! Study it. It may originate from your child, your dog, your cat, your coworkers or even from people watching in a busy coffee shop for a day. Mine for this gold and gather your data. What happens when you're confronted by silly? What do you feel in your body? Does it loosen you up or lock you down? Keep your journal handy, blog about your mission, share your observations on your social media sites, collect your thoughts in any way it seems natural for you. Watch for judgments, physical sensations, emotions…anything you might feel. Do this with the intention of merely observing its effect on you. After one week, ask yourself if there is something you'd like to adjust with your relationship to silly.

SERIOUSLY? ADULTS AREN'T SUPPOSED TO PLAY

Is there something that stops us from allowing ourselves to play? Perhaps various factors are involved, likely deeply ingrained in our subconscious. What are our belief systems around the concept of play? I was a little shocked recently when somebody shared a beautiful creation they had hand-made, and another person's droll response to this was, "Wow. You have WAY too much time on your hands." What triggers a person to say such a thing? Is it a feeling of loss? Perhaps they feel they don't make the time, so their response is to armor themselves with judgment about another's so-called *frivolous* creativity. Is the underlying belief system that creativity is indeed frivolous? Who feeds this thought? Families? Societies? Workplaces? Our own sub-personalities who drive us ceaselessly? The next time someone shows you something they created just for fun, how would it feel to go over the top with support, as a show of solidarity for play? To exclaim, "Wow! That is so awesome! Incredible! How did it feel to make that?" means somewhere inside of us we're giving ourselves permission to do the same, just create, for fun.

Can we be free and bold in our decision to make play a part of our world? Is fear a factor in our ability to open up and let loose? It can be frightening to conceptualize what it takes to step out from the crowd and be an individual who expresses purely without the safety net of conformity. There are those with whom we don't feel safe. We can't express purely, we believe, in their presence. Now consider those who do allow us to express purely. They celebrate our creative steps, our pure expressions of joy, without judgment or scorn. How fun it is to be in their presence! Being the Fascinated Observer means we have the ability to discern with whom we can and with whom we can't play. There's nothing wrong with recognizing our community, our tribe and choosing not to expose our souls to those who don't speak our language. But oh, how freeing and expansive it feels to find others like us, others we can spin with, celebrate with. There's nothing quite like it for me. Having to play by another's "rules" doesn't feel like fun to me. Making the conscious decision to play authentically or play within the guidelines of another person's belief system is our choice.

WHEN WAS THE LAST TIME YOU INDULGED IN FRIVOLOUS CREATIVITY?

A few days ago, Nina told a story about her granddaughter who likes to lie behind the couch with her back on the floor and legs extended up, propped on the back of the couch, toes pointing to the ceiling. She enjoys this new perspective. Nina exclaimed, "Such freedom! Where can we just enter a home and place ourselves in this position, for a new perspective?" I told her she could do it at my house, though I have a polished brick floor that might feel a bit cold and stiff, I joked! But simply hearing those words, even if she had no plan on taking me up on it, felt freeing to her! Do we give ourselves permission? Do we give others permission? These are important questions. We speak in energy. We don't have to say anything at all for a person to feel that we are granting them complete permission to be authentic, even if that may appear silly, frivolous or illogical. When we detach from the expectations we place on others in demanding they behave like us or think like us, we can stand back and watch the fireworks ignite! A soul outwardly expressing is like watching an entire pod of spinner dolphins exploding above the surface of the water.

Do you have a tendency to obsess over another person's approval? I believe we've all gotten stuck here, fearing we didn't say the right thing or do the right thing, feeling left to stew in our own disapproval. Excessive worrying about offending another means we cease to allow ourselves to express purely. Nina shares an example of this, an understanding delivered to her in the form of an email correspondence. She recently sent an email, nothing of great magnitude, but she didn't get a response to it. Nothing. She became confused. Was it something she said? Her mind started picking through the email, searching for that potential social error. Days went by, still no response. A little bit of fear crept in. "What did I do wrong?" she questioned. Basic self-evaluation is never a bad idea. But she could find nothing that made sense. She shifted into the Fascinated Observer and understood that she was attempting to control the outcome of the correspondence. When we send an email, our belief is that we should receive a response in a certain period of time. There was nothing wrong with her words and she knew they were written with the energy of love and enthusiasm. She had to surrender the need to control the outcome of this correspondence! She wasn't playing anymore, she was forcing. So, she gave it to the quantum field. Within a few more days she received a lovely response. No issue at all. It was only her need to understand the other person's rules of play that caused her the mild distress. There is a lot of power in telling yourself, "I did the best I could," if indeed we did and we mean it and then allowing it to leave our energy field and detaching from the need to control another person's response to it. "I did the best I could" when all Four Essential Qualities are activated is the kindest practice of self-love. When interacting with another, are we projecting our fear into it? Or are we implanting potential into the quantum field? For me, seeking outside of myself leads to helplessness. We can't control another person's response. By choosing the philosophy of S.T.A.R. we choose to impact the field, not control it, as we act. I can only express as the seed I plant within myself. If

I plant a seed of fear, I become fear. If I plant a seed of potential watered with *Wholeness (human divinity), Self-love, Play (the now moment)* and the *Embodiment of the Expanded Golden Rule,* this is what I become. I become joy.

Activity: Child's Play

Go get a great big activity-coloring book. Or a sticker book, a puzzle, a model airplane, whatever your heart desires! Spend an hour or two (or three or four!) of one afternoon immersed in the great fun of this simple pleasure. Do this with the intention of mindfulness; stay in the present! When thoughts creep in like "This is silly, a waste of time" or "I have too much to do," gently bring your awareness back to your activity. This activity is about investigating the possibilities!

1. Set a timer for your play session, so you don't talk yourself out of quitting too soon.

2. Consider making this a habit, a shorter session daily or a marathon session weekly.

3. Chart what happens in your life as you continue this practice. Do you feel yourself getting more creative?

4. Do innovative ideas come through in your play sessions?

5. Are you simply more relaxed and open?

6. Perhaps at first you find this highly stressful, and that's okay! Surrender the stress and choose to play anyway.

Gather your adult friends to color pictures with crayons or tinker with building blocks. Feel what happens in your body when a group of adults engage in child's play. We encourage you to be as childlike as possible. The point of this activity is to be light and silly!

PLAY TO CREATE

To manifest is to create. To create, we set an intention. Rather than surrendering entirely, detaching from vision, intention means we visualize the feeling we're searching for and then give it to the field of potentiality. Peruse any book store and you're likely to find scores of titles focused on the ideas of manifestation, and indeed this is the very foundation of S.T.A.R. Accepting our own divinity as creator beings means we are open to the concept of manifestation. "We create our reality" has been written thousands of times over the past few decades. Are we tired of hearing it? Or are we really ready to believe it?

Manifestation is the process of pulling our visions and dreams into the physical realm. Isn't that the formula for innovation and creativity? The lives of Martin Luther King Jr., Julius Caesar, Helen Keller, Albert Einstein, Hedy Lamarr, Oprah Winfrey, Amelia Earhart, Alexander Graham Bell…and millions more, tell us that there have been sovereign beings on this planet earth since the dawn of time. Those who dream, believe, allow and birth into creation some new thought, object or event to change our history, perhaps our very existence, are all around us. The person manifesting the change can be invisible too, their dreams having nothing to do with changing the course of history or inventing the next big thing. They're your neighbors, your coworkers, your mechanic, your dentist, your postal carrier. Manifestation didn't arrive when Esther and Jerry Hicks channeled Abraham or when *The Secret* hit the shelves. Both sources will tell you that this phenomenon has been in our presence since the Big Bang possibly set the wheels in motion to form the Universe and ultimately us as humans. It's in our very DNA, it would seem, to create and manifest.

Do you recognize what you're capable of? Do you allow for it? There is no doubt that our beliefs can interfere with our ability to bring our dreams into the grand light of day. Lee Carroll channels the entity Kryon in his book,

The Twelve Layers of DNA to remind us of the belief that in this holographic Universe we have all been everyone else. What if the so-called junk DNA, (the over ninety percent of our DNA that is not coded), holds the key to our own belief of our manifestation potential? What if it's possible that our very DNA holds cell memories of past lives and past experiences? Lives in which we existed fully confident and fully capable of navigating any new experience or possible danger? Carroll tells us that we have the ability to call to action our very DNA, to activate cell memories of our own knowledge, buried deep within our cells. Imagine! Without triggering a dualistic discussion of science vs. metaphysics, let's pretend for a moment that this is possible and play around with the idea.

DNA is just sitting there inside our cells, right? We may as well ask it to be useful and answer some questions! Let's pretend for a moment that we've been every expression of every human being present on this planet. We've been the rocket scientist, the author, the painter, the expert public speaker, the master chef, the builder…And all of these experiences we've had are stored right there in the DNA of our cells. Now, clear your mind, get into a quiet space and focus on your cells, visualizing your DNA as being tiny audio receptors tuned into your voice and only your voice, just waiting for you to draw upon its myriad resources! Ask it anything! If you're worried about a presentation you're expected to give this week, ask to tune into that part of you who's been the master presenter in some other lifetime! Ask it to infuse you with the past-life experience you've already garnered in this area. Unsure about how to navigate a tumultuous phase with your teenage son or daughter? Then tune into that part of you who knows exactly how best to communicate through this phase. You've done this before! You know! This is a practice that requires no great preparation or perfect circumstance. You can do this in an instant, no matter where you are or who you're with. Have fun with it and see where it takes you.

DREAMS AS SOUL THINKING

Perhaps in my life, the most powerful form of play has come in the realm of dreaming. When we began to organize our thoughts for this section on dreaming, we asked ourselves, what are we talking about here? Is it the fantasies of daydreams, the freedom of night dreams or the active visions for our life? We quickly came to the conclusion that the energy of this section is what empowers all three. It's about what fuels it all, the permission to dream outrageously in any form, waking or sleeping. In *I Will Not Die an Unlived Life*, one of my favorite books, written by Dawna Markova, to which I give partial credit for teaching me how to dream, she writes, "Bear with me. I've been thinking of my soul recently. Soul thinking won't follow a straight line." Her words capture the simple essence of this section on dreams. Are dreams in any form a version of "soul thinking?" It is true that dreams rarely follow a straight line. They are generated from somewhere deep underneath the layers of our identities, roles and beliefs. Our dreams give flight to our very souls.

Author and medical intuitive Carolyn Myss, in her book *Defy Gravity*, writes these foundational words: "Human nature has this fundamental design: We are made to pursue the mythic course of our own lives, to seek out and follow our own greatest quests. This desire we all share is an archetypal appetite to transcend the ordinary, because along with the burning need to share our limitations we are also discontented with the mundane aspects of our life. We are predisposed to find the normal and ordinary uncomfortable, even to disdain if it becomes overbearing." Is this true for you? In your own life, do you welcome the power of mythology and magic? Do you feel you desire it? We are meant to be great; we are meant to be huge beings of light. Can you dream it?

Our dreams can be a portal to mythology and magic. They can feed that human desire to transcend the ordinary. If we all didn't have this fundamental design, then the concept of superheroes wouldn't be the colossal industry it is in our culture. How are your dreams asking to lead you to your own super-powers? How are they inviting you to freedom?

SHHHH!

Silence can deliver the invitation to dream. Do we allow ourselves enough silence in our world? Some of the greatest innovations have been born into the dream stage through the silence of meditation or sleeping. Jogging, taking a solo drive down a solitary road, taking a long hot bath or even waiting in a tedious line, all of these have birthed incredible ideas, creations and understandings. Stillness can help us to hear our own internal voices, and yet that process can also be a little frightening at times.

Sometimes when we try to do something new in life, something outside the realm of our own normalcy, the internal voices start roaring. The ego becomes terrified. There are no neural pathways built for this *newness*. How is it supposed to keep us safe…alive? But our spirit persists, because safety is not what we're looking for; aliveness comes with risk. We're explorers by nature, seeking new territory when life becomes too small for us. Like a hermit crab outgrowing his little shell, we continue, and the voices become louder. Our ego spins visions of annihilation and non-being and death. "Turn back!" our fear tells us. "It's not too late!" it pleads. But when the spirit is dreaming at the helm, there's no staying small. Adventure is our lifeblood and we continue to walk forward, into this new dream, into the practice of comforting and loving our fears with all of their needs for "survival." We finally reach that next solid footing, where our fearful nature can breathe again, until our soul decides to push on again and the silence brings us our next directive. This is the process of dreaming our soul's evolution, which is the byproduct of granting our own permission to expand into something new.

PLAYING WITH SPEED BUMPS

We often say that the S.T.A.R. philosophy is simple, but that doesn't mean it's always easy. There may be a multitude of speed bumps buried deep within your psyche keeping you from connecting fully to the scope of this understanding. And that's okay! Your journey into this S.T.A.R. system is one of illumi-

WHAT STOPS YOU FROM LIVING YOUR MOST PRECIOUS DREAMS?

nation, expansion and growth. Wherever it takes you is unquestionably perfect. Energy blocks are very real and incredibly influential. If the skeptical voice inside of you is saying "Hooey! I don't believe any of it!" or the timid voice inside of you is saying "I just don't trust that I have the capacity to manifest anything," then our guidance to you is to love each and every voice present. All of these voices make up our inner community and each sub-personality inside of us is present for a valid and useful reason. As a form of self-love, it's a compassionate exercise to learn to dialogue with all of our inner personalities in order to come together more harmoniously. There we find new levels of peace, internally and externally and that, my friends, is truly fascinating.

CHAPTER ELEVEN:
DREAMING INTO LIFE

IN NEW MEXICO, I VISITED THE TAOS PUEBLO AND HAD A casual conversation with an incredible artist who works with clay. She spoke of the spirit of the clay and how it was that her intention may be one thing, but after sitting with the clay for some time, it takes on a life of its own and morphs into something completely different from her original intention. She may have a plan, but ultimately the clay has other ideas! So, her message was, as a team, she and her clay dream a piece into living form.

Activity: Molding Life

Go to the kid's section of your favorite store or your local art supply store and pick up some Play-Doh® or other air-drying sculpting clay. Set aside sacred fun time and space to play. Recognizing your medium as a living being, allow the clay to dream your hands into action, creating a small piece to life. Whatever comes through, feel its preciousness as an aspect of you!

- When you are finished, write or tell a story about its origin.

- Who is it representing?

- What is its purpose being born through your hands?

- What is this creation here to teach you?

You may wish to keep the little clay being as a sacred talisman to remind you of your own dream power of creation. Or perhaps return it to Mother Nature, allowing your dreams to take root, by burying your little being in the earth.

Pay attention to what feels right and create your own ceremony around it.

IMAGINING AND RE-IMAGINING

Dreaming our new growth into existence doesn't mean we have to have any idea how it will unfold. Robert Moss, author of *The Three Only Things: Tapping the power of dreams, coincidence and imagination*, writes, "The greatest crisis in our lives is a crisis of imagination. We get stuck and we bind ourselves to the wheel of repetition, because we refuse to re-imagine our situation." In dreaming our desires, the fuel for re-imagining comes in the form of S.T.A.R.

○ We *Surrender* to the power of the desire for a new expression. This is how great change is breathed into existence. When our spirit issues the directive for something new, our fear can't hold us back. Surrender is the first step to harmony when our desire is battling our ego/personality.

○ We *Trust* that our dream is fueling us. We trust that our intuition is guiding us. We relinquish our need to control the outcome to the field of potentiality, which will often deliver an outcome unlike anything we can imagine. By opening to all possibilities, even outside the scope of our consciousness, means we create a much larger opening for potential. Why limit ourselves?

○ We *Allow* the feeling of the manifestation of that dream into our own physical being. We imagine what it will feel like when that dream is a reality.

○ We *Receive* the medicine of the dream, through our process of permission, having released the need to control the outcome of our desires.

When we ask ourselves, "What would it feel like if..." and then fill in the blank with any dream that we would like to manifest, feeling the process work through us, taking shelter in our own body, we are working to build new neural pathways. These new pathways create new ways of processing, imagining and growing into the changes we are dreaming. Without granting ourselves permission to step into something new when we crave it, our life can become as stale as recirculated air. We live recycled ideas, recycled patterns, recycled thoughts. It can feel like old energy dying to transform.

Does full permission to dream in any form come with the full acceptance of our own sovereignty? We believe it does. If we are divine sovereign beings, do we worry about not being "good enough" for our dreams? Do we worry about not being capable or worthy? No, we don't. We allow ourselves permission to dream. We give the dream and our intention for it to the field of potentiality and we choose not to wrestle with expectation of outcome, knowing that the Universe could very well deliver a result much greater than our own capacity for dreaming.

In my lifetime, I have developed superpowers within my nighttime dreams. I can escape any danger. If I am being chased or run down, I can disappear, I can fly, I can walk through walls, any outcome is within my reach. So a few years ago, I had the ultimate understanding of the meaning of this delivered to me by the perfect dream adversary.

In the dream, I was being pursued. I was in a large tower-type home. I kept escaping up every level, evaporating, disappearing, bi-locating, floating, flying, everything I've taught myself to do, and still he pursued me. I was physically exhausted and emotionally terrified. *Why weren't my powers working?* I was mad with fear. Finally, I arrived at the top level. There was nowhere else to go. I surrendered. Knowing he would be here any moment, I shut the door quietly and curled up in a small bed, pulling the covers over my head, softly crying, so confused that I couldn't outrun this guy. In my dark cocoon of blankets, I heard the door crash open. I felt the floor shake as he ran to me in the small bed. So terrified and yet still I lay there, curled into the tiniest ball of defeat I could master. Suddenly, the blankets were ripped off of me and I felt a strong man scooping me up in his arms. As I looked in his frightened face—a large

American Indian man—he said, "Thank God I found you! I've got to get you to safety. This building is on fire!"

That which had been pursuing me, in wakefulness and slumber, I had so masterfully adapted to avoid and outrun, was my soul's evolution. That dream taught me about surrender, and it was delivered to me right after I had left the field of veterinary medicine and had so many fears of the great changes to come, the vast unknown. It was my own blueprint for the concept of manifestation and through it I understood the power that was available to me, if I could only learn to direct it with intention rather than fear. With the foundation of S.T.A.R., we have learned that play and dreaming are the ingredients to manifestation.

THE MAGIC WAND

If we could learn to get out of our own way and believe that we are capable of just about anything—the basic concepts of the human potential movement—would we learn that we are already a lean, mean, manifesting machine? We manifest every day and just don't give ourselves credit for it. We say it's chance or it's luck or "just a coincidence." How about owning it every now and then? It's more fun! And we invite you to believe that if you do, the concept of your own sovereign power will permeate your consciousness and you'll find more and more amazing stuff to take credit for every day.

We say that S.T.A.R. is a magic wand for the sovereign being because it is a tool for recognizing manifestation in our own life, and the Four Essential Qualities are a tool for opening to receive it. It's really pretty simple.

Surrender—We can surrender any belief that we are helpless in our own life, the passive ingredients of "luck, coincidence and chance," knowing that we are infinitely capable and open to creating and receiving the limitless bounty of our full divine potential. We surrender any habits we may have of giving away our power to others while claiming our own ability to be the architect of our life. Recognizing where in our life we are being asked to surrender is a first step to recognizing our own manifestation potential.

Trust—We can trust that as divine, sovereign beings we do have the ability to make things happen in our world, including miraculous things of limitless scope. We can learn to trust that when incredible things take place, the mind-blowing stuff of synchronicities and spiritual epiphanies, that we in some way orchestrated it. Trust is powerful fuel for all forms of spiritual expansion and it's important for the recognition of our own manifestation potential.

Allow—We can allow for new ways of being and thinking. Though we may be troubled by limiting belief patterns in our life, we can open to new possibilities, allowing our minds to expand into a new place of awareness; that place of *beginner's mind*. By opening to all possibilities, knowing there are so many mysteries to be explored and discovered, we open to our own soul-flight. Allowance is key to manifestation.

Receive—And finally, when we've surrendered to our own self-made obstructions, invited trust, welcomed allowance, we can fully receive. Receiving means recognizing that there are gifts all around us, alighting upon us softly as a butterfly, and it's within our ability to see them everywhere. Receiving means that when magic happens in our life we *recognize it* as magic. Once the recognition takes place, the entire Universe seems to conspire to dazzle us. Receiving is the act of bringing that dream into the physical realm. It's the gift of manifestation in myriad forms.

If S.T.A.R. can prime us to recognize our own manifestation potential, then the Four Essential Qualities can help us open to receive the concept. The two together are a simple blueprint for implementing manifestation in your own life.

Wholeness (human divinity)—When we accept that we are divine, creator beings, we know that we are capable of creating that which we desire in our lives. It's not up to anyone else to launch us or hold us back. We are the supreme masters of our progress and purpose. Nothing that happens to us can derail that; our circumstances can bring knowledge and experience that has the capacity to make us stronger, even if that means we're crippled momentarily.

Self-love—It takes self-love to open to the place of empowerment needed to navigate manifestation. This may require a journey of healing to get to a place of pure self-love, but we can begin to open to the concept with the simple intention to do so. If we are coming from a foundation of self-love, then we mirror to the Universe that we are open to receiving more of that love. Coming from any other foundation—fear, hate, frustration, etc.—means we are likely sending out a beacon of that same frequency, which works to manifest more of that into our field.

Play (the now moment)—We open to receive the energies of manifestation by remaining in the moment. Creativity happens in the present. For powerful allowance, we may think about the intention for something in the future, but we meditate on what it feels like in our body right now, as if it is a present reality, in order to imprint in our bodies to that which we're opening. Feel the joy of it, the elation, the expansion, the freedom, in this very moment, happening in the space of timelessness. Let your physical/emotional feelings be a beacon for more of what you want. When the words, "I can do this!" erupt through your energy, pure joy flows unimpeded. This is where manifestation dreams and lives.

Embodiment of the Expanded Golden Rule—Because of the undeniable influence of the interconnection of all things, this state of being can be an enormous power source for our own manifestation. When we set our intentions based on the wellbeing of all earthly creatures, our own passion and purpose become clarified. When we hurt others, we are ultimately hurting ourselves. When our dreams support the ultimate wellbeing of the very planet we need to thrive, we send a dual message to the Universe: *I care for others and therefore I open to the possibility that the world cares for me.* To connect with this essential quality means we manifest with impeccability.

INSPIRED INTENTIONS

With every new experience, S.T.A.R. inspires us to step with intention. The first time I (Kristy) facilitated a group coaching conference, I was terrified. For a month before the launch I dialogued with the voices inside of me who argued I wasn't ready because I was too afraid. What gently led me out of my fear was the process of connecting each and every day to the concepts of *Surrender, Trust, Allow, Receive* as well as to that pillar of the Four Essential Qualities which was shaky. For me, it was *Self-love*. So, that frightened voice inside of me, so terrified to stand in front of a crowd, reminded me that what it needed was just a ton of love and compassion. I had to develop ceremony and ritual around my intention for the class, which was to help others connect with their own manifestation potential and learn to work with their energetic blocks. I had to transcend my own blocks in order to help others in transcending theirs! When I connected with that intention, purely connected with my own passion and divine purpose, I was able to tune into a higher octave within myself. The fear dissipated because I listened intently to that part of me that was so afraid. I allowed other parts of me that weren't afraid to come into the dialogue, to comfort my being and allow my strengths to shine. I had to set an intention that I find comfort in this new experience. Without that intention, I don't believe my group coaching experience would have launched. Intention is our rudder; it faithfully serves as direction in our life.

In our own quest for strengthening our manifestation muscles, intention is crucial. If we have no idea where to begin, for example, we can simply set the intention to begin the process. We tell ourselves, "My intention is that I connect with the four pillars" and then *Surrender, Trust, Allow, Receive*. We make our choice (to connect), we command our own field and then we hand it to our own divinity and wait for the response. We have all the ability right there inside of us.

Intention can be the fuel for three variations of manifestation, which we call *powerful intention manifestation, pure intention manifestation* and *well-intentioned manifestation*. As we go on to describe the differences, look for examples of these in your own life to connect more deeply with their meaning.

Powerful intention is the stuff of the well-practiced master of creation, though we're all capable of it through design. We're born masters. When we can impeccably connect to the philosophy of S.T.A.R., powerful intention is the natural response.

One example of how this type of intention flows effortlessly into manifestation is the brief story of how I (Kristy) came to be the co-author of this book. It began when I met Nina Brown at a wellness center in Santa Fe, where I worked in the front office and she was a client. I quickly became fascinated by her and looked forward to those moments we had together before she was seen for her appointments.

A few short months later, she gifted me her book, *S.T.A.R. Philosophy,* asking me to take notes and keep track of any important insights the reading inspired, as well as questions it may have elicited. Grateful for her faith and trust in me, I casually opened the literary gem not knowing it would pull me so powerfully through its quantum portal. I loved it! I dog-eared nearly every page, highlighted nearly every sentence and filled the margins with questions, comments and exclamation points. Having a master's degree in transpersonal psychology and a private practice in transformational coaching, I was no stranger to spiritual writing, but this one permeated me. I saw its potential in holistic form.

When we met for lunch to discuss my thoughts on the book, I was so excited my heart was racing. I wasn't even sure why I was having such a physical experience. I explained to Nina my thoughts, aspirations and dreams born from the experience of reading this book. I launched into the big vision, where this could take humanity, which seemed to be what the book inspired in me. After about fifteen minutes of my ebullient babbling, Nina casually picked up her phone and said, "I wonder if the Universe will play with us in this moment?" and dialed. The next thing I knew, I was on the phone with a book publisher. After a fifteen-minute interview, I was asked to co-write Nina's next book. I said yes with no hesitation.

Fifteen years prior I had had a prophetic dream in which I was told that I would be publishing my first book at an exact age. That dream had driven me and guided me for over a decade. Right before I had met Nina, I was aware that

my book was progressing slowly and that the prophetic age was approaching. I might not be fulfilling
my own prophesy! I tried to reconcile and attempted
to let the dream flow into the field of potentiality,
surrendering to the Universe my expectations while
trusting in the process. Falling straight from the sky,
a manifestation born of love and passion, *The Fasci-*

**CAN YOU SEE
A FASCINATING
STORY INSIDE
YOU THAT HAS
FORMED INTO A
FIRM BELIEF?**

nated Observer had chosen itself to be that first book, answering the call of my
own intention. I fully allowed it to be published during the exact year of my
prophesy. I could never have predicted this scenario. Never knowing what a
connection will bring, remaining open to all possibility allowed me to manifest
Nina and this incredible book project.

In *Return of Love to Planet Earth*, Nina Brown tells another incredible
story of powerful intention in action. Several years ago, utterly consumed by a
ground-breaking plan to launch a medical wellness center, Life Sustainability
Group, LLC, a new medical model based on a higher expression of awareness,
she stepped into a new phase, one in which she needed to believe in miracles.
This was so far outside of anything that had been attempted before. She wrote
that her first cosmic step was to let go the reins and allow the shedding of her
defenses. No stranger to hard work, Nina has a decorated history, which includes
an appointment by President Bill Clinton to represent him at the White House
Conference on Small Business and shortly thereafter being chosen as a charter
member of Pennsylvania's Best 50 Women in Business. So, this vision of hers
was no pipe dream; she was fully committed to bringing it to life.

Along with her two partners, a part of her grand vision included a division
of the clinic for advanced neurosensory diagnostic equipment to be included
with internal medicine, pharma-genomics and other cutting-edge alternative
medical modalities. Jumping through all of the requisite hoops in order to be
validated and accepted by Medicare, she was informed that she would need to add
a certified audiologist to the staff for the neurosensory division to be approved.

Having no clue what this even was and hearing a cacophony of naysayers
tell her she'd never find one in New Mexico, she took a look on the internet

and found one in her state. She sent an email to him and then released her intention to the field of potentiality, something that had become as commonplace as breathing to Nina. She relinquished control, knowing she had been granted one month to find this person and plug them into the grand scheme of her revolutionary medical vision. They would present, she just knew it and she let it go. Because Nina is a manifestation master, it came as no shock that within a few hours that very same day, this certified audiologist contacted her. He told her that his vision for his professional future was directly in line with that of the Life Sustainability Group. He had gotten word of her advanced medical equipment which, he said, complemented the direction he wished to take in his own practice. He was enthusiastic to meet with them right away.

Though other factors contributed to the eclipse of the manifestation of the Life Sustainability Group, one division of it, the S.T.A.R. clinic, an inter-dimensional, intergalactic construct which admittedly left Nina's business partners a bit baffled, actually manifested into the physical. Alas, the idea for the neurosensory diagnostic division was ultimately rejected by Medicare and the dream of the wellness center was aborted. To Nina, it was obvious that she was not to fill out Medicare forms for the rest of her life, but to move off in her current direction. These incredible events serve as a mind-blowing testament to the power of intention. Nina is a walking example of the mastery of manifestation.

The second form of intention manifestation is *pure intention*. This is the classic example of people doing superhuman manifestation feats based on an incredibly powerful and generally life-or-death intention. Several bystanders witness a mother literally lifting a car in order to save her child pinned underneath. Impossible, right? Nothing is impossible when pure intention is activated. Other examples of miraculous manifestations from pure intention include Tibetan monks levitating stones, Hindu saints transforming water into milk, Moses parting the Red Sea—all metaphors for the pure manifestation born of agony or ecstasy. It's also the fuel behind those miraculous stories of people healing themselves of terminal illnesses and leaving the medical establishment dumbstruck, and family members finding each other after years of separation through war or natural disaster.

And thirdly, *well-intentioned manifestation* brings to mind the vision of Walt Disney in the film *Fantasia*. In the third segment of this film titled *The Sorcerer's Apprentice*, Mickey Mouse portrays the apprentice, who through innocent intent, creates a whole new version of reality. This is what we refer to as the wildcard intention, possibly asking for something we haven't fully considered. It can also be the challenging aspect of manifestation, here to remind us of the power of our thoughts in what can sometimes be a dark delivery.

An example of this is something I (Kristy) think of frequently. Years ago I was standing in the backyard of one of my best friends, Shari. It was a small gathering and to my sister, who had never been there, I was thoroughly explaining a sad event that had happened a few years back in which a giant, ancient oak tree had been destroyed in a straight-line windstorm, which devastated the area. Losing the tree was heartbreaking. Shari recalled that this magnificent tree is one reason why she and her husband bought the house. Always empathic with nature, I began explaining to my sister, Jill, how losing the tree affected the family, truly feeling the grief of the loss and transmitting the energy so powerfully that she began to tear up. I cried too. We connected to the tree, the other trees left behind and the effect its death had on the entire neighborhood. We stood in silence for a few minutes, in the very place the tree used to stand, pondering what it must have felt like for that giant tree to tear from the ground, and then we went inside for dinner. Within thirty minutes, we heard a thunderous crack, an explosion, and watched in horror as the tree next to where we had been standing, blew apart for no apparent reason. There wasn't a breeze present; it was a bright sunshiny day and the limb on the silver maple tree was gigantic, no small twig. With no warning, the tree sent its dense appendage crashing down onto the patio, completely decimating a brand new patio table and chairs set. Had we been sitting there, well, I shudder to think if we could have scattered in time.

I froze, kind of horrified, because I immediately recalled the conversational depth to which my sister and I had gone, feeling the truth of the past oak tree crashing down, knowing the power of human thoughts. Had I caused this?

Shari, the stunned homeowner, looked right at me. "Why did that happen?" was the first thing out of her mouth. "I don't know!" I replied, still somewhat horrified at the possibility of the answer.

The next day, my friend called a professional arborist to come clean up the destruction and evaluate the tree. There was no explanation for the anomaly. The tree was in complete integrity and there was no evidence of previous stress or strain to that particular branch. One of those unexplainable phenomena; he just scratched his head. To this day, I believe that we went into such empathic depths, connecting to the fallen tree, that the Universe believed we were setting an intention. We became it, we felt it, we lost ourselves in the truth of that fallen tree, entered a place of timelessness, and being sorcerer's apprentices in that moment, didn't fully grasp the enormity of our communication. The field of potentiality doesn't judge our intention as being "good for us" or "bad for us." Sometimes, it just delivers.

Activity: I Know What to Believe

Write down all your beliefs about manifestation. Keep writing until you've exhausted your inner voice. For example:

◎ Manifestation happens with others, but it doesn't happen with me.

◎ Sometimes I question if there is such a thing as manifestation.

◎ I read something that said manifestation is a bunch of hooey, so I'm afraid to admit I believe in it.

Your beliefs may be affirmative too, but look for any doubts or questions that may hold you back. Then write what you believe to be any possible limiting consequences of your beliefs, such as:

◎ I don't believe it happens with me, so therefore I feel inferior.

◎ Questioning the presence of manifestation means I can't ever create it.

◎ If I admit I believe in things like manifestation, I may be labeled a wacko and I can't risk that.

Now, take all of the beliefs you've uncovered and write the Universal opposite of your beliefs. For example:

○ I am a divine sovereign being with powerful manifestation abilities.

○ As a divine creator being, I fully accept the gifts of manifestation.

○ My own beliefs are not dependent upon the beliefs of others. I honor their beliefs and I honor my beliefs, without fear.

Feel in your body what it feels like to say your Universal statements out loud. Spend time with these feelings, truly allowing them to permeate your body, mind and spirit. Connect to these statements of expansion regularly to note what starts to shift in your life.

EACH MOMENT A NEW INTENTION

Each and every day, we cycle through all three phases of intention manifestation, depending upon the moment and the circumstance. The human experience is delightfully unpredictable and that's what makes it so rich. Bringing into our consciousness our intentions for manifestation sets the foundation for exploring our full potential. Manifestation is pure magic. Our choice to pay attention to it in our life can be outrageous fun. Perhaps the purest foundation of S.T.A.R. can be found in play, dreams and manifestation. We have to know how to play to dream, and we have to dream to manifest. Keeping it light, not taking ourselves too seriously, giving ourselves permission to play and dream and create—these things bear the very fruit of daily miracles which happen all around us.

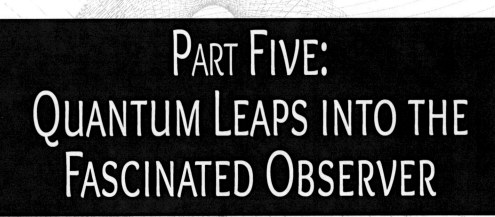

PART FIVE:
QUANTUM LEAPS INTO THE
FASCINATED OBSERVER

BELIEF AND COURAGE

From *S.T.A.R. Philosophy* by Nina Brown (page 159)

Wisdom is knowledge or information that has no emotional charge and has been accepted as personal truth, which allows us to align our will with the will of the divine Creator. When we have accepted information as simply being our truth, it becomes our belief. We have faith in what we believe in, which gives us courage to act on this innate wisdom. When we have faith and courage in the *S.T.A.R. Philosophy* and take action, we reprogram our brain and move into a new identity of self. Our power then moves within to reinforce the courage we need to be this new identity.

When we repeat that uncharged thought and add another, we begin an inner alchemy process or ascension process, of raising our frequency. As our belief about who we are changes, so do our actions, because our new belief gives us courage to behave in new ways.

CHAPTER TWELVE:
THE MASTER FASCINATED OBSERVER

PURPOSE HAS A WAY OF CONNECTING WITH US. It's a soulful calling, a gentle prodding. People have traveled the world in service to their purpose and have initiated profound change in their life by realizing what they believe they were called to do or be. Purpose is always there, right there, inside of our heart, mind and soul, waiting for the spark to ignite it. It never looks any one way or speaks any one language. I believe that our purpose is guided by our divinity and that everyone has it. None is superior to another. No purpose is nobler than the next or more or less beneficial to the planet. Our purpose is the connection point to our own divinity.

When I (Kristy) was in my twenties and early thirties, I was haunted by my purpose. I literally felt it stalking me, like an entity. At the time, I had no idea what to make of it, this unsettling sensation, but told a friend that I felt like some ghost was trying to reach out to me to make contact. I was a little afraid, but did everything I could to accommodate it. At the time I was utterly confused. I held séances with myself, in the dark with a candle lit, paper and pen in hand, hoping for some automatic writing which could explain this pull on my heart, this urgency in my soul. I didn't tell anyone of my desperate attempts to make contact. They'd think I was crazy, I assumed. But just beyond the veil, just beyond the reach of my senses, was someone or something scratching and clawing at the barrier between worlds in an effort to reach me. It took a vision of my own soul disconnecting from my body and my horrified attempt to stuff it back in for me to realize that this being that was trying so desperately to reach me was my own soul purpose. "What does it want with me?" I pleaded in my solitude, not having any idea what I was supposed to be doing with my life, but knowing it wasn't this…that which filled my days. The urgency intensified. It was only when I had another vision of me publishing a book years later that my purpose was finally able to take seed. And that seed within me grew into the most disruptive mighty oak, which tore through the earth and my reality both in order to reach the light of manifestation. I allowed it to take place, this perceived destruction, because I knew from my own spiritual discernment, that this was just all part of the process preparing me to write and fulfill my purpose. Now, I had a level of peace inside of me to pacify my fears and uncertainties and unrest, a level of peace that was directly connected to my own soul calling.

Imagine that we came into this existence with an agreement, a contract, we had signed with cosmic dust—a contract between our soul and our source. For a moment believe this is true and contemplate the following:

- What is your destiny?

- What have you written into that agreement?

- Do you believe this agreement could be guiding you, compelling you, urging you forward?

Listening to our inner wisdom, our inner voice is what connects us to this calling. Our calling links us to the divine. Connecting to this inner knowing means that we will turn on a dime if we have to and completely alter our life in an instant, if the time is perfect and the conditions are ripe for us to heed our own calling. Our purpose can gently whisper or roar like a lion. It does what it has to for us to hear it. But when we do hear it, honoring it can mean a leap of faith into the wild unknown. It can mean the severing of things we've outgrown, lessons we've mastered, rescinding tired patterns, making space for our deepening into the life that fills us with our own capacity for creation. It may mean we look for new connections with those who can foster our purpose and find new relationships which support our rapid growth.

Saying goodbye to those things that no longer serve us can feel like a death of sorts. Nature has her way of clearing ground so that newness may emerge. Buddhist author, Joan Halifax, writes in her book, *The Fruitful Darkness*, "When we sever ourselves from society in a rite of change, there is an invisible door that we pass through that has no words on the other side." She goes on to say, "If it is the door between life and death, we sacrifice our physical body and if it is the door of initiation, we sacrifice our social body. This door also separates

and joins the living and the dead. Creation requests that we open this door."
We open this door, an initiation of sorts. We open the door right into our own
living soul, connecting the living and the dead, which are right there inside of
us. I truly feel that the beginning of my own initiation into my divine purpose
was the feeling that some *dead thing* was trying to reach me. I have come to
connect this dead thing to that part of me that had become so disconnected it
felt bereft of life. I had to bring myself back to life through my own power of
creation, administer CPR to myself through dreams, visions, mystical experiences and my own perceived craziness. Looking back, I wouldn't change any of
it. The joy and anguish—all was perfect.

Our intention can spark our purpose. If we sincerely have lost awareness
of our purpose, we can set the intention to reconnect. Simply commanding the
field to open us to our purpose is a powerful beginning.

Like breadcrumbs leading us through the dark forest, our purpose is clearly
connected to our passion and our joy. There is no trace of dread or obligation
or boredom when we talk of the dreams that are in alignment with our soul.
Though we may confuse accumulation of money with the accumulation of richness, in truth it has little to do with how much money we make. Millions in the
bank won't pacify us when we've disconnected from our purpose. In fact, many
of those who have made material conquests their sole meaning in life, without
a connection to their soul contract, spend a good portion of the time fearing
their loss of it. The great question is, what do you love to do? That's the biggest
clue to understanding your soul contract. It's been said that purpose is where
your passion meets the needs of the world. Where is this intersection for you?

I met a janitor of an elegant high-rise glass and steel building in Minneapolis years ago. He emitted such a frequency of happiness and joy, that I was
curiously drawn to him. I asked him, on a long elevator ride up, what had him
so jazzed today? "Life." He answered. I continued to engage him, drinking up
his effervescence; I wasn't having as good a day myself. He told me that his
vision was to clean up the world. Every day, he would engage his soul contract
(though he didn't use that terminology) by getting out of bed at an ungodly
hour of the morning to get to work by four o'clock a.m. He would visualize the

entire world becoming sparkly clean through his efforts in this one building. He honestly believed it to be true. And hearing him, I did too! I left that building feeling the spark of his purpose and the power of his intention. I left that building feeling that he had somehow cleaned up my energy field! It fascinated me to wonder what had brought this to pass; what had caused him to come into this world with this divine contract? I could only speculate, but what a joy to witness a man so connected.

Some folks move with grace and ease directly into their purpose and in fact, with some, it would seem they were connected to it from the moment they took their first breath. Others aren't always so certain. In fact, connecting to the full octave of our individual purposes created some serious chaos in my life and Nina's both. That's okay; it happens in a person's life just as they have orchestrated it. For me (Kristy) personally, I had to let go of my material existence before I could move on. It looked like destruction. It felt like freedom. It was also terrifying. Scientist and visionary Gregg Braden writes in his book *The God Code*, "Nature shows us that to move from one level of order to another requires a period of chaos in between. It is from the collapse of an existing pattern and the ensuing chaos that a new pattern and greater order may be found. To borrow from the popular metaphor of the 'calm before the storm,' this time of chaos may be viewed as the 'storm before the calm.' Whether we are talking about the chaos of divorce that precedes the happiness of a new marriage or the layoff from one job that leads to a whole new career, each benefit is preceded by a time of unsettled change."

In fact, our purpose is so divinely ordered that it can orchestrate our spiritual emergence. A person's reintegration into a life of spirit nearly always brings with it a sense of healing or helping something in this world in need of their loving attention. For some, a spiritual emergence is a gradual immersion into their own role as a creator being, a divine spark in this vast Universe. We never lose our connection; sometimes we just need to *remember* it. For others, their emergence happens all at once, so powerful as to break through the iron walls of resistance or fear into the wild ride of a spiritual emergency. Christina and Stanislav Grof, authors of the transformational book, *The Stormy Search for the Self*, write, "During a spiritual emergency, the logical mind is often bypassed and the colorful, rich world of intuition, inspiration and imagination takes over. Reason becomes restrictive and true insight takes one beyond the intellect. For some individuals, the excursion into the visionary realms can be exciting, spontaneous and creative. But more frequently, since it does not involve states of mind that they consider normal, many people assume that they are going crazy." I did. I wondered if I was losing my mind. It's a common thread in an experience millions have navigated before me.

The sometimes-sudden power we feel when we connect to our divine purpose can indeed make us feel like we're breaking free from consensus reality. Perhaps we need to in order to truly get to know ourselves. Internal whisperings or roars, when coming from your own soul connection, are not crazy or unattainable. Our purpose, our passion, they are for us to define, not consensus reality. Some fit right in. Others have chosen a unique expression. Our purpose, our divine spark, is not subject to the judgment of others, nor are we here to judge another's. No matter how big or small, outlandish or nondescript, we can hold the divine spark of those around us in sacred space and expect our own to be nurtured in return.

When a person is connected with their soul contract, their divine purpose, they light up like the North Star. Others feel it, they're inspired by it and are drawn to it inexplicably. They may know nothing about a person, but when they enter a room, it glows. This, they can feel. This, they want to understand, get to know, be closer to. Because this is something they recognize within themselves—that glowing, that *something* that happens when our purpose is ignited. It's a beautiful, magnificent, godly thing.

I want that connection. How about you? I feel it takes an element of mastery to consistently stay in that quantum field.

MASTERY OF CONNECTIONS

Mastery of connections is like child's play. A child under three can be a master of connection. A child can move from laughter to tears in a flash. Unlike adults who tend to process analytically before allowing emotional expression to occur, children can easily express without stopping to analyze anything. For example: "I have a lollipop. I'm so happy!" Next moment, "Whoops, I dropped my lollipop in the dirt. I'm so sad!" The connection to that moment and what the child is experiencing is all that exists. Dogs are also masters of connection. For example, if you hold a delightful treat in front of a dog's nose, I guarantee you they are fascinated by, "That smells good. I want to eat it. When will I get it?" Nothing else exists in that moment except the idea of eating that treat. And if you offer a dog a treat the next day, the enthusiasm level does not diminish; they are just as excited the second time. The child would also be excited the next day to receive another lollipop. The point I am leading to is that the child and the dog are models of what it means to master connections. Mastery of connections means that we are fully in that moment experiencing with fascination the totality of all that is occurring.

When we are being who we are, connected, without fearing the acceptance or the rejection of others, we are liberated and free to express our purpose. We can live this way when we're connected to our own hearts. Self-love is the strongest foundation. Living and expressing from our hearts is effortless when we have a foundation of self-love. It flows and moves our energy like silk. To an outsider it might be perceived as courageous living, but when we're connected to it, we know it has nothing to do with courage. It's simply who we are as divine sovereign beings, expressing our truths with fascination.

A man walks down the street. He smiles and says good morning to everyone he passes. You know this type; he may catch you off guard in your own morning aloofness. You haven't had your coffee yet. You turn slightly and mutter hello back to him, though he's already passed by. This man, he maintains eye contact with everyone he meets. He really means it when he says, "Have a good day." You *know* he means it. Is he afraid of rejection? What if someone ignores him or doesn't return his well-wishes? What if someone thinks he's strange? Or worse! What if someone's actual response is to fully reject his gift of presence with an early morning F-you? What if? This man, he honors the responses of others, no matter what their expression. He's living from his heart. He knows that other people's responses have nothing to do with him. He won't stop handing out his *good mornings* because that is what he desires to do—connect with the hearts of others, no matter how the other is expressing him or her self. To a person who fears rejection, this simple way of being may seem like the epitome of fearlessness. But to ask the man…it's just his way. There's no forethought or conscious effort involved. Perhaps it started that way, with a little fear. Maybe he even practiced it. But by this time, it just flows. It's his heart talking. No repression needed, because he's not invested in the outcome. He's giving his gifts and isn't motivated by what he receives in return. This is the Fascinated Observer in mastery.

When my (Kristy's) nephew, Noah, was around two and a half years old, he was over the top cute. He has always been highly introverted. In contrast with his round little toddler belly and rosy cheeks, he had this dignified no-nonsense air about him. He was an old soul hanging out in a tiny body. It was priceless. We used to call him the little Buddha. One day he was riding around in the grocery cart, his feet dangling through the little openings, hands tightly grasped around the stability grips, minding his own business. His inner world was rich and fairly private. He wasn't smiling, just observing; the little guy seemed deep in quiet meditation. But everyone who passed him this day seemed to go out of their minds, poking at him and talking in baby talk, which never seemed to thrill this tiny Buddha. Finally, he met his threshold. A woman saw him, threw something in her cart and dashed over to fuss at him. She thrust her face right next to his, literally poked his belly and shrieked, "How are you, little man?!" With the calm of a master, no expression on his face, he quietly replied, "No. Go away, please." The woman laughed and retreated, didn't take it personally. His mother was a bit horrified, but my nephew had reached his limit! It was becoming painful. At less than three years of age, he may not have been skilled at the concept of enduring this form of torture for the sake of polite sacrifice. He did say "please," after all. But to this day he's highly introverted and thinking back, that must have been an extremely uncomfortable experience for him. Why *would* he believe he needed to endure it endlessly? In that moment, Noah had mastered connection. He remained true to himself, his spirit and he did the best he could to protect this woman's feelings. But he didn't repress his spiritual and psychological needs.

Think of how often we dismiss our needs. We're at a party and we want to be home reading, but what would our friends think of us if we were home by eight o'clock on a Saturday night? We're at work enduring another discriminatory joke, when really we feel like if we ever have to hear another joke at another person's expense a part of us will literally die inside. We're afraid to tell the person to "Go away please" because how will that be received? We crave a dance class, something really invigorating like hip-hop, but we feel we're too old and too fat. So we repress the desire and sit on the couch watching a dancing reality show, alone with our potato chips. What will it take to give voice to our own precious hearts? What would it take to spoil us and give into whatever our heart wanted, without repressing through fear and denial? Staying connected means we don't stay mute to the detriment of our own soul.

Mastery of connection can also mean creating a new relationship with uncertainty. What happens when we befriend uncertainty? When we do, the Fascinated Observer stands up and takes over. So often in my (Kristy's) work I'll be elated, having so much fun listening to a client bubble over about some magical thing flowering in their life. I can just feel their energy giving flight to our conversation, infusing the entire atmosphere with the energy of a fully expressing life. It's intoxicatingly beautiful and something to which we all have access. Suddenly they pause and instantaneously the energy shifts. "But I'm probably just crazy," they say, "or I'm setting myself up for failure or something. I mean, in a month this could all just go away and I'll be right back where I was, miserable." Boom. The expansive energy evaporates. They've lost their connection and here we are, back in the same old story that has kept them unfulfilled. The Fascinated Observer doesn't fear the "what if's" of a month from now, because through the process of *Surrender, Trust, Allow, Receive*, we can learn to let go of our expectations in exchange for our intention. Without the attachment to expectations—what if I fail, what if they reject me, what if I look weird, what if I'm wrong—we can remain connected to our experience, fully connected, living from our hearts, not our fears.

What does it take to stay connected? The junction point is where our divine presence and our human experience meet. This can be thought of as the reunification point, where we once again become a unified whole. Mastery of connections happens in this place. Disconnection is understandable in our culture. Zen Buddhist author, Jack Kornfield, writes in his book, *After the Ecstasy, the Laundry*, that we repeatedly encounter a lack of respect and nurturance in our society and even in our very families. He says, that through "the judgments and fears of those close to us, the inevitable frustrations, loss and cultural fragmentation that trying to meet society's expectations brings, we begin to separate from our own sacred body and our deepest feelings." This can take place in the hidden realms, unconsciously, and though we can sense our disconnection, we may not know exactly from what or how it may be remedied. We simply start to drift away from our own connection.

In our world many do consciously or subconsciously choose to disconnect. I have heard many a client tell me something like, "At age nine I decided that I would never trust another person again as long as I lived." A child's intention is strong when born of pain and hurt. After spending decades stifled by a state of constant mistrust, we may find, not surprisingly, that the Universe throws us reason after reason to believe that human beings are untrustworthy. Often when we finally get it, something clicks in our consciousness. Understanding that we are creating this dynamic in our world, we can, as sovereign divine beings declare that it's time for a new experience. And we receive it, by connecting to a new intention as strongly as our nine-year-old creator self did to the old one.

The truth is, connection can be painful and we are taught to avoid it in our culture. When we have a headache, we take something to make it go away. This extends to our spiritual life as well. But closing off because of the pain—wearing permanent psychic armor—means that we also close ourselves off from much of the ecstasy. Trust is critical here. Although S.T.A.R. makes a nice acronym, maybe in your life trust comes first. Perhaps for you trust comes before you can surrender, and understanding that about YOU is mastery.

Trust is so important in finding our connection to our junction point, because opening to a place of connection means we're opening to a place of experience and being that might be downright uncomfortable, painful even. Maintaining our connection in the face of discomfort is indeed mastery.

Have you ever met a person and thirty seconds later you can't remember their name, but you're too embarrassed to ask them again? Perhaps we're too concerned with how we're appearing to them to be able to hold them in our own attention? Or maybe we're lost and drifting in an experience we had four hours ago, so present in the past that we can't anchor in the present. It very well may be that there is no singular reason or focus, that this is simply our everyday state of mind now, completely fragmented and ungrounded. Talk about painful. Very few enjoy this feeling. Connecting again is a journey that can take place in an instant, though. Like a snake shedding her skin, we can let go of the fear that keeps us disconnected. All at once, it can happen like this, we can open to a new intention of presence.

When a person has a peak experience, a singular event in which the embodiment of their divine nature in spirit form ignites, it can change their life in an instant. So instantaneously, in fact, that there can be a feeling of grief or loss when they *come down* from such an experience. We've heard people say, "I don't feel like I belong on this earth" or "I just want to go back home to the spirit realm." Perhaps you've even said or thought something similar. This life can be an intensely painful place to be; just knowing that it is serving us by indicating where we are disconnected can bring peace.

Such a painful disconnection can arise when we lose our footing from our junction point. Living only in our divinity means that we temporarily lose touch with our humanity. We are on this earth to express the form of human experience. We came here to feel these magnificent bodies, in pain and triumph. We came to feel the full spectrum of emotion, to use our senses and expand on them, possibly pushing our species' very evolution into the territory of something new. We did not come here to be numb to our own glorious nature. Wholeness requires the human experience, while staying connected to our divinity too—and that is a precious opportunity.

We commit to the junction point (the place where our humanity and divinity meet) in limitless ways. A sacred contract, we understand that this is nourishment for our soul, which brings purpose or fulfillment to our human form. We meditate. We pray. We ride horses. We paint. We play guitar. We write math formulas a mile long. We walk in the woods. We go to a baseball game.

Some may require ceremony and ritual, others may require no structure at all. There is no right or wrong; no path to the source of heart and soul is more or less powerful than another. The intention of staying connected, staying whole is unobstructed, awake and alive.

DIVINE CREATIVITY EXPRESSIONS

A best friend of mine, Ann, recently fantasized about a new endeavor, which was a strategy to bring mindfulness to the teenage population as a way to help them cope with the tumultuous angst that can sometimes accompany this life stage. She wanted to help them cultivate their own spiritually creative resources. She was so excited. But then she paused and asked, "How do I know if I'm doing this from my place of divine purpose or if I'm doing it from my ego? I mean, I might just want to be *the* person that does this for the teenage population." The answer was important for her and it's a great question!

The answer is, does it matter? Both are imperative. The ego is a part of us. When creating from the junction point, when our divinity is activated, we can't do wrong. The ego is welcome when our spirit is driving us.

Doubt can be a killer for us. "Am I doing this from a place of ego?" means we've taken our divinity out of the equation. We're assuming *we don't know*. Our spirit doesn't ask questions, it knows our intention is pure. To take our judgment out of it, we make a declaration by saying, "I choose to undertake this spiritual creative project in alignment with the will of the divine." We surrender to that and we invite ego into it. That's right—in this case ego is included. Some incredible things have been accomplished in this world when ego and spirit meet at the junction point. When balance is achieved and divine intention is activated, integrity permeates our work. If we're creating from the junction point, we can be sure we're creating from the heart.

A simple tool for discerning our motivation for our creative work is to bring the question of intention into it. What is your meaning behind your work? What's driving you? It's easy to tire of our creative projects unless a larger purpose is behind them. Consider this:

○ We are driving from our divinity when *intrinsic* value (what we receive internally, like joy, peace, excitement) is activated.

○ When our motivations are driven by *extrinsic* value (what others will provide to us for our work); the associated value will likely wane with time because the ego/personality usually is driving our actions.

How many stories have we heard of those who placed all their value on the extrinsic—we stockpile money, never having enough—only to find that our mad rush for more, more, more, isn't satisfying us any longer. Inside of us is a bottomless pit that never fills. *Citizen Kane*, which film critics argue very well may be the best movie ever made, was the classic story of this very phenomenon. The beautiful and most famous movie ending of all time finally revealed the origin of Kane's dying word, "Rosebud," and we wept for the magnitude of such a haunting climax. If you're one of the few people who hasn't seen it, watch it tonight! It's the story of intrinsic versus extrinsic power, distilled into black and white cinematic brilliance.

I don't know Ted Turner personally, though some may call him a modern-day Citizen Kane. But there's a facet of this billionaire communication mogul's divine creative expression that is public knowledge. Having lived in remote northeastern New Mexico for two years, I came to know a roaming herd of magnificent buffalo, which amble about the wild frontier in that part of the world. They are a private collection of mammalian souls in Ted Turner's care. Turner buys up millions of acres of frontier land across New Mexico, Montana and Wyoming as a creative project that seems to drive his soul. It's certainly not about extrinsic value for him. What he says is that he's attempting to restore the West to what it used to be, before the days of Buffalo Bill. As a part of this mission, he's trying to restore the genetic purity of the buffalo, as well as many other projects involving the grizzly bear, the black footed ferret and land conservation. I don't begin to know the extent of it, but when I look at this, the project appears to be driven from his junction point, though only Ted Turner knows that for certain.

I can make up my own story about it and that is that his motivation is to give back to the natural world, to make an impact, to see a difference...who knows; it's only conjecture. But what I see is an enormous canvas, this project, with an enormous history behind it. A history he's trying to undo. He's painting a potential new outcome for this species, the buffalo, and he's painting it with the color of his own purpose.

We don't have to be a billionaire mogul to see this in our life. One glaring example that we can see every day is our fascination with blogging and social media, which extends across the world. Read any book on blogging and there will be giant warnings posted throughout about the importance of finding intrinsic meaning for your work. The internet is littered with abandoned blogs, which began as exciting ventures, a platform for a person's greatest expression, but which quickly lost steam because not enough people commented or contributed, leaving the author feeling dejected and empty inside. Why? Because they lost sight of their joy, which was the reason for doing it in the first place and became sidetracked by their need for approval and popularity. This happens to all of us, it's our nature to want to connect and spread our love and enthusiasm.

The point is, we can run forever on the battery of our own divinity, but when we start expecting others to fuel our battery for us, well, we're going to run dry. Are we beginning an online presence about inspiration in order to be popular, which we'll judge only by an uncountable number of comments and feedback to our words, which are sure to make an impact on the lives of millions? Is it fair to quantify our divine purpose like this? Or are we starting an online presence because we want to share the joy that the energy of our divine creative expression infuses within us? Do we want to do this primarily because it will make us feel happy and fulfilled and satiated? If so, there's an inexhaustible supply of that inside of you. You'll never run out of "juice."

If in our creative expression, we're hoping and waiting for people to love us—and constantly tell us so—we've become disconnected from our divinity, lost contact with our junction point and may have inadvertently wandered into the disconnected ego, rather than the connected ego. We can't sustain our creativity in the realm of the disconnected ego. It's painful and disappointing there. Our extrinsic expectations rule in such a place.

Master artists will tell you they create for themselves. If people love their work, wonderful! But that's not why they create. As soon as they start saying what they believe people want to hear or painting flowers because that's what they believe will sell rather than their soul's inner landscape, they cut themselves off from their own power supply. Most find their connection again; it's what the masters do. They know that our creativity is divine when we do it because we love it. It flows from our heart's joy and nourishes everyone it touches when it's born of our soul. There is such power behind it, the blending of our entire being.

In every one of us lives a feminine and masculine aspect. In our world though, it's easy to become unbalanced. We cast our feminine Eros (which can also be thought of as creativity) aside for our masculine Logos (which can also be thought of as logic), or the reverse may be true. Collectively our culture has become unbalanced in a patriarchal sense; logic trumping feeling. Over the past several hundred years it has seemed as though the Divine Feminine has truly taken a beating across our world. But there is evidence all over the planet that this balance is being restored; we are becoming more creative, more intuitive, more empathic to everything around us. True power is expressed through the balance of these two godly forces—male and female. The awesome unbridled creative force of the Divine Feminine when coupled with the limitless strength and drive of the Divine Masculine is an unbreakable combination. Welcoming the synergistic union of both into our life brings unfathomable resources. We connect with both inside of ourselves, and then we bring them out into the world.

In my (Kristy's) own life I reached a point where I had nearly killed off my own feminine without being conscious of it. In my corporate job, I came to believe that femininity meant nothing more than stiletto heels and the perfect shade of lipstick. Meanwhile my ambition and drive ran roughshod over my own creative force for years until, like my sweet nephew Noah, I reached my threshold, only mine was more explosive. It resulted in a ten-day spontaneous mystical experience through which all of my suppressed psychic receptors blew open at once. The force of my feminine creative re-entry nearly killed me. I awoke one morning knowing in that moment that I could choose, right here right now, life or death. Had I chosen death there would be no repercussions.

I would have just drifted silently away and my husband would have found me dead in our bed, the autopsy would have revealed no explanation. This is how I saw it at the time. I chose life. And my whole world changed.

I believe that the purpose of this mind-blowing experience was to re-introduce me to the magnitude of our own creative power, our divine creative expression, which is inside of us at all times. And it became my purpose to foster it.

MASTERY OF OCTAVE SHIFTS

Octave shifts are ways of perceiving in our world. We like the word "octave" because it's free from dualistic thinking. When making the shifts we do not judge where we are as higher or lower consciousness, instead we understand that wherever we are is perfect and is simply part of our journey, so we declare that there is no better or worse; one octave is never superior to another. Shifting octaves is a way of communicating our choice to be present with what we are experiencing without shying away from it in fear or shame or altering our experience to make another person feel more comfortable or accepting of us. It's about being the Fascinated Observer *in and of* our own lives, rather than labeling events as good or bad and struggling within the confines of limiting stories. Octave shifts are about accepting whatever presents as a divine opportunity, no matter what disguise it's wearing.

Recently an incredible woman by the name of Kathleen shared her brief story with us. We receive a lot of magical S.T.A.R. stories, but this one seems to truly align with the focus of this section. The story began with an account of Kathleen falling on the ice, breaking her ankle in three places. She lay on the frozen ground that grey winter day waiting for an ambulance to arrive, all the while feeling no pain and repeating a mantra in her head over and over, "I am one with the All-Prevailing Healing Powers of Love!" Setting up this experience through her energetic octave proved to be miraculous. Though originally informed that it would likely take plates and screws and wires to fix her shattered ankle, she healed so quickly that the doctors chose to monitor her progress non-surgically. She became one of only five percent of people who were able to heal from fractures this severe with non-surgical intervention. Following is what she wrote about what set her up for this masterful experience.

Kathleen's Fall into Grace

Late last winter I received a message through dreamtime, three times in one week. It was very clear and very simple. The message was this, "*Surrender, Trust, Allow, Receive.*" Since those messages came during the week of my birthday, I took it as a special gift to use as a focus tool on my path of unfolding and I found it to be very, very useful as I went deeper and deeper into the alchemy of my inner work. When I first received it I had no idea how to make use of it. However, staying willing, my inner guidance opened a gate to a pathway rich in resources readily available for the asking and I learned to apply what I called a "S.T.A.R. light tool" as I moved forward. Fundamentally, it was about learning how to be consciously present in each *now* moment. The answers to my original questions such as "What does *Surrender* mean to me in this context?" "*Trust* what or whom?" "What am I being asked to *Allow*?" and "What will be *Received*?" shape-shifted many times as I progressed through life's offerings. However, one thing definitely remained constant, which was how I felt when I took the time to apply the S.T.A.R. tools. Truth be told, I felt lighter and less dense, more comfortable in my own skin, my thinking was clearer and I was more at ease with the process of change overall.

Then, just before the Winter Solstice, an author and book was brought to my attention that just plain "flipped me out!' That author was Nina Brown and the title of her book was *S.T.A.R. Philosophy*. This magnificent text is a handbook to Higher Consciousness and an invitation to "step up to the plate" and claim our true identity as the Sovereign Creators of our lives, remembering ourselves as the Divine Beings that we are so we can make manifest our Golden Age of Divine Love.

It was a masterful account of what we're writing to express. Not once did Kathleen write about how badly this sucked for her or how it was going to inconvenience her. Indeed, it sounds like she flipped into an immediate place of acceptance, claiming her own divinity, before she even hit the ground! No drama, no "poor me," nothing to thwart her body's ability to deal with this internal chaos peacefully and masterfully. She found the gifts in a broken bone and she used them to her advantage. She got out of the way and let her body get to work, doing its thing at a divine level, which is what it's built to do.

The invitation is to hold the intention to be the master of the drama in all things, as Kathleen so beautifully grasped in this story. Buddhist author Lama Surya Das writes in his book, *Buddha Is as Buddha Does*, "At the innermost, secret, level of our being, we remain connected to the eternal energy flow of the Universe, the indefatigable, dancing rhythm of life. Realizing this inexhaustible higher power within us fills us with trust and confidence. Heroic effort at this level keeps us in touch, through *prajna* wisdom, with the bigger picture, the long-term view and helps us avoid getting hooked into dualistic reactivity and taking too hard the momentary disappointments and setbacks and obstacles along the way." At this octave of being our flow is effortless, without goals, expectations or demands. And yet we may be fully committed to healing, whatever that means for us, through our intentions. Being the Fascinated Observer is not about disconnection or inactivity; it's about mindfulness. Without mindful intention, we may dissociate from our divine purpose.

Recently one of my best friends had a brief scare, which she quickly shifted into an octave out of the reach of fear. Lynn, my friend, is a cancer survivor. Coming through the tumultuous experience of Hodgkin's disease, she has done extraordinary work reconciling with the forces that she believes set the stage for this experience. She hasn't vilified the cancer or made it into some all-powerful monster ready to strike again at any moment. She's done her hardest to befriend it, realizing that her painful near-death odyssey through this experience made her stronger than she's ever been. Friend or not, however, she lives with some lasting health challenges from the chemotherapy and radiation with which she continues to dialogue.

Recently, surrounding one of these issues, she pulled an oracle card to gather new insight. The card read, "Storm's Coming." She immediately went into disaster relief mode. "Oh my God! Storm's coming! This is bad, really bad…" and then let this reflexive voice trail off. She calmed herself. Closing her eyes and coming to a place of inner wisdom, she asked herself the meaning of the card. It was a reflection of that part of her still ready to fight or flee. It was a mirror to show her that there was still a part of her afraid, in need of love and caring. She immediately shifted into a new place energetically. No more fear. Just love for her body and the changes it was going through.

When we master our own octave shifts, we move into that place of effortless flowing. We lose our connection to the *story* of things happening "to us," and we begin to accept our awesome place in this Universe. In making this transition, we see how everything in our life is a tool for our evolution as spirit, including those things that can be classified as drama. Our consciousness is luminous, that is to say, it illuminates or lights our path. When that luminous field is "on," we see how our thoughts can flow to a place of strengthening our journey. We light our own way.

Mastering octave shifts means that we allow a wider scope to our experiences. Rather than getting caught in a limiting story, we expand into a possibility with every interaction we have. When we become the Fascinated Observer, we don't take a pre-fabricated story into our every experience. We stop filling our minds with thoughts of speculation and conjecture about others with motivations for which we can't possibly own or take responsibility. We can create awful destruction in a person's life in the name of "I know what's best for you." Only *they* know what's best for them. Only we know what's best for *us*. When we ask for advice, we're inviting another's perspective, and we may truly need it. But we must maintain our own connection at all times rather than handing our power to another or expecting to have power over another.

As I (Kristy) neared the completion of writing this book, I had an experience with my dog that blew me wide open. I thought it was *one thing* and it turned out to be completely another, on a different dimension entirely. In the beginning it rattled me. To set the stage, I have had Saluki dogs for twenty years.

They are otherwise known as Egyptian greyhounds and are considered a rare breed originating in the Middle East. They are known to be the oldest living breed of dog and for me are incredibly karmic. They connect me to my Egyptian soul-lineage and we have always had powerful connections. For example, my Salukis have always developed the exact health issues I have had and vice versa. It's like our bodies mirror each other so we can help each other heal. It's incredible. Recently this mirroring became visible with my dog, Arya, a young five-year-old beautiful little soul.

I have always had a crooked tooth on my right side. This tooth represents many things for me. If I were to go into story about it, it would represent my fear of lack. Growing up, my family was very poor and couldn't afford braces. In America, who hasn't had braces? The story this tooth can represent for me is that "I'm poor" even though today that isn't the case. I frequently dream that this tooth falls out and it feels so good! Well, my belief is that Arya picked up on that frequency. One recent morning I woke up and had a strong intuition to check Arya's teeth, for no reason in particular. To my horror, her right side canine tooth, the exact equivalent of my crooked tooth, was dead, indicated by an odd color it had turned. I knew the meaning of that discoloration from my many years spent in veterinary medicine. I went into a kind of panic. I didn't make the octave shift. I saw this in dollar signs. I was going to need a board-certified veterinary dentist to remedy this with a root canal, something which would likely cost thousands of dollars. I fretted about it and immediately whisked her off to the vet.

Immediately upon seeing the vet we determined the tooth was the least of her issues. Blood work revealed that her liver was failing. Not in any way connected to the tooth, but both issues were expected for dogs many years older than Arya, so now we had another mystery. Here's a dog who eats organic food, who spends most of her day curled up on the couch, seemingly deteriorating in front of our eyes. I was terrified and heartbroken. And the tests continued.

Working with both a holistic Eastern medicine veterinarian and a traditional Western veterinarian, I wanted to cover all bases. Still no definitive answers with more tests. There was no explanation for why her liver was failing, a potentially life-threatening situation. So, Nina asked me one day, "Why don't you hire an animal communicator? Ask Arya what this is all about." My mind went blank. Why hadn't I thought of this? I know several! I was in such a "Get out of my way, I'll take care of this with my mind" mode, that I had completely taken Arya out of the equation of her own healing. Serendipity chose the communicator I'd use and I called her immediately.

Arya's issue turned out to be nothing I had considered and more powerful than I could imagine. I figured since my own personal naturopath was working to detoxify my liver and adrenals and since my Salukis always share my own physical issues, that she was just trying to help me detox my own liver. She brought me to a much deeper level, this little soul-partner of mine. The communicator revealed that Arya's soul was "on the fence" about being here or not being here. Though she lives a sheltered, loved and cherished life, her soul is intensely sensitive to the world and living in it was much harder than she had anticipated. She hadn't yet connected to her divine purpose, which is every bit as important to an animal as it is to a human. Through an hour of work, including healings by Anubis and Sekhmet themselves, Arya made the choice to stay in this world and thrive.

But, Nina asked me the next day, *had I?* Taken aback, I wondered what she could mean. I recounted the story of the last section, when I was given the choice and chose life. But *had I*, truly and entirely? If Arya was mirroring my physical reality, was she mirroring my spiritual reality too? On some dimension, was I on the fence?

Through this powerful revelation, I made the declaration to Arya that I was fully committed to this life. And she committed to me the same. Making the declaration, though I was previously unaware that I *needed to*, was intensely powerful. I felt more grounded, stronger. Allowing Arya to take control of her own healing allowed my own healing to take place on a level that was so deeply hidden.

So, this wasn't an "Oh, woe is me, this is costing me thousands of dollars" moment. It was an invitation to navigate this experience from my heart, with the illumination of my full consciousness. Arya is a sovereign being too. She made the choice to engage in her own healing process and made the commitment to connect with her healing lineage, her divine purpose. With a few months of a rigorous liver detoxification process combined with some energy work, Arya's health is strong today. Her liver values are completely normal and her tooth is actually regenerating!

Our conditions aren't punishments; our experiences aren't payback. What if they are simply opportunities for making our next octave shift? The Bible reads in John 9:2, "As Jesus passed by, he saw a man blind from his birth. And his disciples asked him, 'Rabbi, who sinned, this man or his parents, that he was born blind?' Jesus answered, 'It was not that this man sinned or his parents, but that the works of God might be made manifest through him.'" Jesus then went on to restore the man's sight. Jesus made it clear that blindness wasn't a punishment or a curse; it was simply a channel through which divinity could course.

OCTAVE JUMPING

How does it feel to translate this to all the challenges in our life? They're not about karmic punishment or retribution for our misdeeds, but mere openings for us, invitations to make an octave *jump* into a new way of being and perceiving all that which happens around us. Don't confuse an octave shift with an octave jump; an octave shift is a gentle transition while an octave jump is a great leap in consciousness. Imagine, in a blink of an eye, jumping from first grade to receiving your PhD. An octave jump is a quantum leap into the field of all possibilities completely freed from any encumbrances that may have once plagued us. We can find our way through the chaos and turmoil when we willingly walk right into it as it shows up in our life, fascinated by the possibilities. As Deepak Chopra says in his book, *The Third Jesus*, "Turmoil is actually a positive sign; it's a symptom of spiritual ferment. In the aftermath, looking inward brings to light all the things we don't want to see. It's not peaceful or calming when we air out the unconscious mind. Fortunately, it doesn't have to be. There are natural mechanisms that can do the work of creating order out of chaos." To us, of course, the natural mechanisms are *Surrender, Trust, Allow, Receive*.

Gandhi believed that the intrinsic goodness in all people was Universal. This goodness inside of each person shines brightly and can be known as their divine truth. Acting in accordance with our truth, which is fed by our universal consciousness, is our divine navigational system. This, connection with our heart as our navigator, is mastering the octave shifts. Keshavan Nair, in his book, *A Higher Standard of Leadership*, wrote that Gandhi "devoted a great deal of his life trying to convince people to acknowledge the good in others, to reject differences based on caste, religion and social position and to work for the welfare of all." His belief that goodness is inherent in all people extended to those who opposed him. He sought to inspire, not coerce or intimidate. His fuel was love, not rage. Few will argue that his masterful methods brought love, nurturing and healing to our world and also initiated great change.

What Is Missing?

Mastery of octave shifts and octave jumps is, on a foundational level, the S.T.A.R. Fascinated Observer. We intentionally left out any exercises in this entire final section because when we reach this level of mastery we no longer need precise instructions. We know exactly what it takes for us to direct our own evolution. People send light into our lives to inspire our actions. The answers magically appear. Our soul leads the way for us. Understanding what making an octave shift means to you, means you can easily connect to the Four Essential Qualities of *Wholeness (human divinity)*, *Self-love*, *Play (the now moment)* and the *Embodiment of the Expanded Golden Rule*. It means you can comprehend a philosophy of observation leading to discernment, rather than leaping directly to judgment. It means you can choose to step out of the limitations of our old stories. Mastery of octaves means finding a new level of freedom. We guard our own locked doors. S.T.A.R. is a key to the octave shifts, a universal key, which opens to unlimited possibility.

After reading this chapter, you know what these levels of mastery mean to us. We now encourage you to define for your life, what they mean to you. Only you can grant you what you need to master your own journey, which starts with the *permission* to believe in yourself. What has this chapter instilled in you? Where have the words taken you? Perhaps you have more questions than answers, and that is perfect too. Finding our own questions helps to free us from all the angst. At this level, all that is required is to open the conversation at the octave of the junction point. There is where we commune with the full empowerment of *Surrender, Trust, Allow, Receive*. From this junction point, we can do no wrong. We are perfect.

FINAL WORDS TO THE READER

Perhaps you're at an octave in your life from which you seek no answers. Maybe you're content with exactly where you are, desiring no insights or guidance, having no drive to stretch into something new. Or maybe you're somewhere very different from there; coming from a place of near-constant searching, a soul on a primary personal mission to connect, grow and evolve as a spiritual being—whatever that may mean for you. It could also be that you're some place in-between, going about your day-to-day, firmly seated in the "reality" of your humanity and yet feeling the gentle tug of your own spiritual stirrings. Maybe there's a small voice inside of you whispering there might be something more. You understand you don't have the answers, but find yourself asking the questions more and more.

Wherever you are, we'd like you to understand that this book was written for you. Wherever we are, we have made the choice to be right here, experiencing all the richness this particular state of being brings to us. Wherever you are, we want you to know you're not alone.

This book was a labor of love, a work of passion, meant to deliver to you a tool for greater connection, to more purely merge with your own being, with those around you and with the greater world at large. We believe you'll walk away from the experience of this book revitalized and ready to spend more time observing your life with an abundance of fascination. Through that experience, we believe new empowering insights will course through your life.

Through the writing of this book, our souls scrutinized our every written word. Were we being congruent walking our walk? Did we truly believe the words we were writing? Were we being honest and transparent and real? To be sure, we were put through actual experiences with each chapter written. The words on these pages aren't just words, they are encoded experiences in literary form. There was a Universal system of checks and balances which went into this creative expression, meant to keep us impeccable with our word. To be sure, we had to live sometimes very painful experiences through which we assisted each other through the navigation, using the S.T.A.R. philosophy. We embodied the pure strength of every emotion and were fully present for each other as we felt and expressed the full force of our pains and joys. This book is a living story and we are the characters, as will you be by the time you read these final words.

I fully expect you to have undergone your own mystical experiences, your own sacred transformation, through the navigation of this living entity in book form. We tell you now that we are here for you, should you need any company through your experiences. *The Fascinated Observer* is about building a new world through sacred communities and divine connections. As a reader of this book, you have entered a sacred and life-long community. You are so welcome here.

Epilogue
Insights from Nina Brown

PHILOSOPHER'S SEED

Philosophy is: the activity through which we see creation through the eyes of the Creator.

The full octave expression of philosophy is about nurturing the seeds of wisdom hibernating in our sacred hearts. We are born with those seeds. The philosopher's stone, that holds the secret seeds to everything, has transformed into the philosopher's seed—a living being which can burst forth into new, never before expressed shapes, forms with playful creativity.

What a journey we have been on! Kristy and I began the experience of writing *The Fascinated Observer* by setting the intention to explore deeply the full octave tone of four words: *Surrender, Trust, Allow, Receive*. We planted this intention as seeds in our individual sacred hearts and nourished them. By means of weekly discussions, the seeds began to grow in fascinating and unpredictable ways. Branches and leaves, which formed chapters and sections of the book, developed as we explored new ways of responding to our life experiences and that inspired us to question how we could apply S.T.A.R. and the Essential Qualities that support the S.T.A.R. philosophy to respond to our challenges in ways that lessened suffering and enriched our souls.

The young plants growing in our sacred hearts began to stretch and push both of us, challenging us to live and feel the full octave tone of the words that we were choosing in each sentence. We were becoming the living book. We were writing from the inside of the book experiencing both physical challenges and the profound emotional upheaval of old belief systems that were crying out to be released. The journey was not always comfortable, but we had the support of each other as we continued our exploration.

Mastery is a process accomplished in octaves. Mastery of the S.T.A.R. philosophy will be an exhilarating life-long process for all of us. As drama, chaos, transitions and the richness of life experiences present themselves, we will choose to see creation through the eyes of oneness, as Fascinated Observers, with appreciation and gratitude. S.T.A.R. has become our magic wand, which we hand to you in book form as a tool for you to use as YOU wish.

It is our vision that the S.T.A.R. philosophy be a wisdom seed in your sacred heart and that it burst forth into new never before expressed shapes, forms and outcomes. Have fun playing with S.T.A.R., the magic wand of the sovereign being!

Reading Resource List

Abram, David. *The Spell of the Sensuous: Perception and Language in a More-Than-Human World.* New York, NY: Pantheon Books, 1996.

Braden, Gregg. *The God Code: The Secret of Our Past, the Promise of Our Future.* Carlsbad, CA: Hay House, 2004.

Brown, Nina. *Return of Love to Planet Earth: Memoir of a Reluctant Visionary.* Santa Fe, NM: Cauda Pavonis, 2010, 2011. ——*S.T.A.R. Philosophy.* Tulsa, OK: Gather Insight, 2013, 2014.

Carroll, Lee. *The Twelve Layers of DNA: An Esoteric Study of the Mastery Within.* Sedona, AZ: Platinum Publishing House, 2010.

Chopra, Deepak. *The Spontaneous Fulfillment of Desire: Harnessing the Infinite Power of Coincidence.* New York, NY: Harmony Books, 2003. ——*The Third Jesus: The Christ We Cannot Ignore.* New York, NY: Harmony Books, 2008.

Connor, Richard and Dawn Micklethwaite Peterson. *The Lives of Whales and Dolphins.* New York, NY: Henry Holt and Company, 1994.

Cori, Jasmin Lee. *The Emotionally Absent Mother: A Guide to Self-Healing and Getting the Love You Missed.* New York, NY: The Experiment Publishing, 2010.

Emoto, Masaru. *The True Power of Water: Healing and Discovering Ourselves.* Hillsboro, OR: Beyond Words Publishing, 2005.

Estes, Clarissa Pinkola. *Women Who Run With the Wolves: Myths and Stories of the Wild Woman Archetype.* New York, NY: Ballantine Books, 1992.

Firman, John and Ann Gila. *The Primal Wound: A Transpersonal View of Trauma, Addiction and Growth.* Albany, NY: SUNY Press, 1997.

Ford, Debbie. *The Dark Side of the Light Chasers: Reclaiming Your Power, Creativity, Brilliance and Dreams.* New York, NY: Riverhead Books, 1998.

Godin, Seth. *Poke the Box.* Do You Zoom, Inc, 2011.

Grof, Christina and Stanislav Grof. *The Stormy Search for the Self: A Guide to Personal Growth Through Transformational Crisis.* New York, NY: Tarcher/Penguin, 1990.

Halifax, Joan. *The Fruitful Darkness: A Journey Through Buddhist Practice and Tribal Wisdom.* New York, NY: Grove Press, 1993.

Hanh, Thich Nhat. *The Heart of the Buddha's Teaching: Transforming Suffering into Peace, Joy and Liberation.* Berkeley, CA: Parallax Press, 1998.

Katie, Byron. *Loving What Is: Four Questions That Can Change Your Life.* New York, NY: Three Rivers Press, 2002.

Kornfield, Jack. *After the Ecstasy, the Laundry: How the Heart Grows Wise on the Spiritual Path.* New York, NY: Bantam Books, 2000.——*The Wise Heart: A Guide to the Universal Teachings of Buddhist Psychology.* New York, NY: Bantam Books, 2008.

Lama Surya Das. *Buddha Is as Buddha Does: The Ten Original Practices for Enlightened Living.* New York, NY: HarperCollins, 2007.

Lesser, Elizabeth. *The Seeker's Guide: Making Your Life a Spiritual Adventure.* New York, NY: Villard Books, 1999. ——*Broken Open: How Difficult Times Can Help Us Grow.* New York, NY: Villard Books, 2005.

Lipton, Bruce. *The Biology of Belief: Unleashing the Power of Consciousness, Matter and Miracles.* Carlsbad, CA: Hay House, 2005.

Markova, Dawna. *I Will Not Die an Unlived Life: Reclaiming Purpose and Passion.* Berkeley, CA: Conari Press, 2000.

May, Gerald, G. *The Dark Night of the Soul: A Psychiatrist Explores the Connection Between Darkness and Spiritual Growth.* New York, NY: HarperOne, 2004.

Mellody, Pia. *Facing Codependence: What It Is, Where It Comes From, How It Sabotages Our Lives.* New York, NY: Harper One, 2003.

Moss, Robert. *The Three "Only" Things: Tapping the Power of Dreams, Coincidence and Imagination.* Novato, CA: New World Library, 2007.

Myss, Caroline. *Defy Gravity: Healing Beyond the Bounds of Reason.* Carlsbad, CA: Hay House, 2009.

Nair, Keshavan. *A Higher Standard of Leadership: Lessons from the Life of Gandhi.* San Francisco, CA: Berrett-Koehler Publishers, 1994.

O'Donohue, John. *Anam Cara: A Book of Celtic Wisdom.* New York, NY: HarperCollins, 1997

Ornish, Dean. *Love and Survival: Eight Pathways to Intimacy and Health.* New York, NY: William Morrow, 1999.

Pink, Daniel. *A Whole New Mind: Why Right-Brainers Will Rule the Future.* New York, NY: Riverhead Press, 2005.

Rankin, Lissa. *Mind Over Medicine: Scientific Proof That You Can Heal Yourself.* Carlsbad, CA: Hay House, 2013.

Rasha. *Oneness.* Santa Fe, NM: Earthstar Press, 2003.

Schaefer, Carol. *Grandmothers Counsel the World: Women Elders Offer Their Vision for Our Planet.* Boston, MA: Trumpeter Books, 2006.

Seligman, Martin. *Flourish: A Visionary New Understanding of Happiness and Wellbeing.* New York, NY: Free Press, 2011.

Wilber, Ken. *Integral Spirituality: A Startling New Role for Religion in the Modern and Postmodern World.* Boston, MA: Integral Books, 2006.

Zaleski, Philip and Paul Kaufman. *Gifts of the Spirit: Living the Wisdom of the Great Religious Traditions.* New York, NY: HarperCollins, 1997.

Zander, Benjamin and Rosamund Stone Zander. *The Art of Possibility: Transforming Professional and Personal Life.* New York, NY: Penguin Books, 2000.

About the Authors

A beautiful and kind spirit, **KRISTY SWEETLAND** focuses her passions on guiding others through transitions that lead to personal fulfillment. Her professional mastery is in the release, subjugation then transformation of deep blocks associated with fear, self-doubt or unseen patterns which impede life goals and hinder the recognition of passion and purpose. To accomplish  this, she uses her wealth of intangible talents combined with her professional credentials, which include a bachelor's degree in psychology from the University of Minnesota, a master's degree in transpersonal psychology with a Certified Professional Coach certificate from the Institute of Transpersonal Psychology and her ACC credential through the International Coach Federation.

Kristy spent many happy years in veterinary medicine working in coaching/administrative/management roles, which included the mentoring and coaching of her employees on wellness, productivity, personnel issues and efficacy in the workplace. As her purpose blossomed, she fell completely in love with her work's mentoring facets. Led by the call of her soul to follow a seedling of a dream, Kristy bravely left behind what had become her identity—her beloved, secure career in veterinary medicine, to find and express deeper meaning.

Strongly attuned to others going through similar soul-level struggles on life direction, she wanted to serve/guide people through those transitions. Answering that soul-level call-to-action launched her into a series of mystical, immersive experiences that dramatically altered her life, her perceptions and placed her on the path to fulfilling her own destiny. A transformational coach, shamanic healer and intuitive channeler, Kristy now serves full-time as a guide for those on the path of owning and culti-vating their own intuitive gifts. In both personal and executive coaching situations, Kristy cultivates her client's spirit to develop and fulfill dreams. For more than a decade, guiding with grace, love and intuition, she has coached a base of international clients from diverse industries including veterinary medicine, software development, health care, education, law, civil and industrial engineering, publishing, divisions of federal govern-ment and more.

Today Kristy operates her coaching practice from her home base in Northern New Mexico, surrounded by the love from her husband and an entourage of beloved four-legged companions. *The Fascinated Observer*, co-authored with Nina Brown, represents the merging of her lifetime of experiential training, wisdom, psychology and philosophy.

FIND OUT MORE ABOUT KRISTY SWEETLAND

COACHINGTOCOMEALIVE.COM

NINA BROWN, a nontraditionally aged cum laude graduate of Bryn Mawr College, went on to distinguish herself as a pioneer in business. In 1990, she established an investment company to assist women entrepreneurs. In 1995, she was appointed by President Bill Clinton to represent him at the White House Conference on Small Business and, the next year, was chosen as a Char-  ter Member of Pennsylvania's Best 50 Women in Business. During this time, she presented at speaking engagements hosted by the US House of Representatives Field Hearings, the Pennsylvania Department of Commerce, the League of Cities Women's Caucus, Wharton Executive MBA Reunion and the Entrepreneurial Women's Expo, where she was the keynote speaker.

Nina subsequently became a consultant and leader in alternative medicine. Among other initiatives, she collaborated in forming a company to bring neurosensory diagnostic tools to injured veterans who suffered brain impairment in the Gulf and Vietnam Wars.

In 2014, after the publication of *S.T.A.R. Philosophy*, she traveled to India, where she presented before a gathering of more than 2,000 members of the Pyramid Society of Spiritual Scientists. While in India, she took *S.T.A.R. philosophy* to Raipur and Mumbai, and then on to Singapore. Two years later, Life University (http://luglobal.org/about-us/) in India asked to add *S.T.A.R. Philosophy* and its companion book, *The Fascinated Observer: A Guide to Embodying S.T.A.R. Philosophy*, to its curriculum.

Currently Nina serves on the executive board of Pristina Natural, Inc. helping to expand the company's presence across the United States and into Canada and Asia. Her desire is to bring S.T.A.R. philosophy into the realm of business, creating a new model for the union of consciousness and business.

Throughout her endeavors, she has been guided by S.T.A.R. principles, devoting her energies full-time to this sacred spiritual mission. She has found that as the needs of the collective shift, the service asked of her evolves, and this transformative work unfolds.

In addition to writing the S.T.A.R. series, Nina is the author of *Return of Love to Planet Earth: Memoir of a Reluctant Visionary.* Her writing has also been published in *Kindred Spirit* and *Sedona Journal of Emergence.*

Ordering Information

Nina Brown's other books are also available through select bookstores, online retailers and CaudaPavonisPub.com, which also offers quantity discounts for bulk purchases.

RETURN OF LOVE TO PLANET EARTH
Memoir of a Reluctant Visionary

6" x 9"
978-0-9826769-0-5
388 pages
$19.95
eBook: $9.99

Indie Excellence Finalist
USA Best Book Awards Finalist

"What a treat to be privy to the journey of a walking master one who has successfully assimilated all aspects of her higher self."
—Dr. Bali K. Sohi, psychologist

"A must-read for any spiritual seeker."
—Lee Carroll

"In reading this beautiful book you will gain a deeper appreciation for your own life and a greater understanding of who you really are."
—Robert Schwartz, author of *Your Soul's Plan*

The S.T.A.R. Series ~ Book 1
S.T.A.R. PHILOSOPY

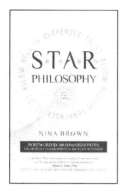

6" x 9"
978-0-9826769-1-2
200 pages
$17.00
eBook: $9.99

"In this book Nina Brown inspires us to embody the 'now' state of being with her expansive comprehension of infinity consciousness."
 —James F. Jereb, PhD
 Author, visionary artist and
 founder of Stardreaming Foundation

"Each page in this book contains a precious jewel of truth."
 —Daniel R. Condron, DM, DD, MS
 chancellor, School of Metaphysics

"Nina Brown's original voice, breathtakingly lucid, sensible, and rewarding as a child's smile, invites us to dance in our human divinity."
 —Jeff Ferrannini
 Internet radio producer

Cauda Pavonis
PO Box 32445
Santa Fe, New Mexico 87594
CaudaPavonisPub.com

CPSIA information can be obtained
at www.ICGtesting.com
Printed in the USA
FFOW03n2332080517
35341FF